About the Author

Jan Amos is an inspirational writer, screenplay writer and healer. She discovered her love for writing at the age of 42 on her journey of awakening. During this awakening she also discovered her purpose in life is to instruct mankind to dissolve the ego within the mind and assist people on how to live from their souls.

Jan has a strong passion to help the youth and has volunteered many hours with the youth in her community in Canada.

Jan is a mother of two beautiful daughters, has many other children close in her heart and has one very special granddaughter.

Dedication

I dedicate this book to my birth children, my two extra children, my stepchildren, grandchildren, step grandchildren, my mom, sisters, nieces and nephew, great nieces and nephew, girlfriends, friends, neighbours, ex-partners, past lovers and my current love. This book wouldn't be the same without the teachings and learnings from each and every one of you. I am extremely thankful for these learnings, awareness and the raising of my consciousness in all our relationships. I can now pass on this knowledge to help improve the relationships in the lives of my readers! <3

Special thanks to Gisele and my kids for being there for me in such a supportive role during the many days of writing this book! <3

Jan Amos

RELATIONSHIPS

TWIN FLAMES FAMILY DYNAMICS & MORE...

AUSTIN MACAULEY PUBLISHERS™

LONDON • CAMBRIDGE • NEW YORK • SHARJAH

A CIP catalogue record for this title is available from the British Library.

ISBN 9781528931281 (Paperback)
ISBN 9781528966610 (ePub e-Book)

www.austinmacauley.com

First Published (2021)
Austin Macauley Publishers Ltd
25 Canada Square
Canary Wharf
London
E14 5LQ

Introduction

So... at the beginning of this book, it's the year 2008 and I would have to say that all my relationships are dysfunctional! Yes, this sounds bad but it's the truth; all my relationships are DYSFUCTIONAL. My marriage is in bad shape, kids not so good, mother difficult, sister pretty bad, stepchildren – we might not even want to go there – neighbours not good and family not good either. Sound familiar??? Unfortunately, this is really what it's like out there. Now don't be too hard on yourselves, you are not alone and truly you are in good company with the rest of us. I would have to say 90% of the world is dysfunctional as mankind has not evolved and really they don't want us too. This knowledge is another entire book in itself.

The good news is time has passed and it's now the year 2019; all my relationships are healthy. I have had a lot of lessons, a lot of growth and it has been work to get here. I now can say that every single relationship I have in my life at this moment in time are healthy ones. These relationships being from my family, to my children, to my friends and to my lover! This book will take you on an interesting journey from complete dysfunction to complete peace within! So hold onto your seats, it's going to be quite the ride.

Welcome

How many different relationships do we really have? Are we ever taught what a healthy relationship is? Right now I am 50 years old, single and I have had many relationships in my life. I am presently a mother, a daughter, a grandmother, a stepmother, a step grandmother, a sister, an aunt, a caregiver for my mom, an employee, a customer, co-worker and a friend. What I have learned is that each and every one of these relationships is slightly different and you need to use different learnings or skills in each and every one of them. Even at times you may have to use different skills and knowledge in one category. As for instance, I have four children in my life and I'm a little different with each of them. As you read through this book, I will explain how I went from unhealthy relationships in most of these areas and how I now have healthy relationships in all of them.

Next I will dive into the love relationship area because I am single at fifty and I have had quite the experiences. These types of experiences are from dating to twin flames, to age differences. It has been a journey that I am finally realising is a good thing as I truly wasn't sure for the longest time why these events were happening to me. Like what was God doing to me? And how could this be happening to me?

Right now, there are so many single people looking for love and to share their life with someone. I hope the pages of this book bring light to the area of the love relationship and all relationships. I also believe that everyone comes into our life for a reason and they are to teach us something and create growth within. This is an important perspective to have.

Mom and Dad

I believe it's always good to start at the beginning and this is going to be with our parents as it all begins with our parents. Yes, good old mom and dad are our first attempts at a healthy relationship. The only problem with this is: have our parents experienced a healthy relationship? Are we entering into a dysfunctional environment? An environment that has been like this for a long time? I have also learned and do believe that we pick our parents before we arrive; therefore, the lessons we have learned from them we have asked for. This might be a hard one to understand but I believe it is the truth.

Our parents are our first teachers in life. In my situation, timing was a large factor in the outcome of the relationship with both my parents. I was the third and last child born to my parents with two older sisters already in place. My sisters were 12 and 14 years older than me, so I guess they could say I could have been an afterthought and that's okay. I am definitely meant to be here and children arrive when they are to arrive. My mom was 36 and my dad 38 when I was born.

Mom: I always had a very close relationship with my mom. It was like a soul partner relationship, like as if we were not to be far from each other. I could tell her anything, knowing there would be some judgment as she was a little old school but she would listen without punishment. We never fought until I was 45 and this was when I was learning to finally stand up for myself. Although I must say she always supported me and was an amazing grandmother to my children.

I had a very bright light when I was born and I am thankful for the love I felt from my mom, as it kept my light shining. As I already said timing, yes timing had a lot to do with the outcome of our relationship. My mom was older and had experienced some growth over the last 12 years since she last gave birth and this helped. I know for sure that it was a rare relationship I had with my mom, as I was a witness to the relationships she had with my two older sisters and they were very different than mine. It was also an extremely different relationship with each of my sisters as well.

9

My eldest sister, April, and my mom had a very dysfunctional relationship from the start to the end. That's the truth of it and it is what it is. April was such a soft soul person and I couldn't understand why my mom was so hard on her but she was. Due to this, they fought a lot. April married her first love and he was not a nice guy and he ended their 10-year marriage when April was eight months pregnant with her second child. She didn't fare well at all and really who could blame her or who would. She became weaker and of course my mom became harder on her. I believe my mom had the belief that you should be hard on your kids when they are not doing the correct thing in their eyes. This may be very true, as there is a belief with kids to be hard on them when they are not doing well. Moreover, I know that my mom's father was like that with her. My mom was repeating the same dysfunctional and hurtful behaviour towards my sister that she had experienced from her father. I wish April was able to find the strength within to survive a parent being hard on you all the time but unfortunately she wasn't. If my mom only knew the power of love and that really the best thing she could have done for April was to love her and love her more when she was downing with the hardships of life. Even though they were mother and daughter, their bond and connection was and remained thin. Because of this, my mom was unable to help April's children at the time of need, which is a very sad thing. This dysfunction that started with my grandfather rippled down to affect his great-grandchildren. April died at the age of 61, just too hard of a life and not much love in it. Love is so important to your health and wellbeing. Love keeps the vibration of your body high and this makes good health within. I remember well the look of peace on April's face as she was lying in her casket and seeing that her body was pain free. It was as if she finally was free and was with the love of God again. My mom was standing beside me when we approached the casket and my mom did cry hard at this time but it was too late.

I did try to explain to April on her deathbed that our mom had a very tough childhood and that she was unable to express love as she didn't receive it as a child. Her parents separated when she was two years of age and she was raised by her dad, my grandfather; both these situation were very unusual back in the 1930s. I reminded April how hard our mom's father was on her and this was something she was passing down to my sister. Now my grandfather was a good man but didn't show much love and never supported my mom with her swimming either. She was an Ontario champion when she was 13 and it was her coach that gave her the support she needed. I know for a fact that we do pass down dysfunction and it is our responsibility to see the dysfunction around us and break the cycle. I know my two sisters and I have loved all our children and gave them unconditional love so we did break this cycle in our family.

My middle sister and my mom kind of had an in-between relationship. She wasn't as hard on Anne and Anne was a much stronger person. Anne and April did not get along at all and this made it hard for everyone. They were just so opposite, Anne was very clean and April not so much. This caused a lot of upset as they shared a room. Anne ended up going to a private school to finish her high school years which ended up being the best thing for her, as she went into nursing and found the love of her life to which she is still married too. Although near the end of my mom's life, her and Anne's relationship didn't really bring out the best in each other. There was a lot of judgment placed on my mom for how my mom decided to live her life in the end. An unnecessary judgment from my perspective, as there really is no room for judgment. We are all on our own journeys. Anne had a belief in how my mom should live her life and because it wasn't fulfilled, she chose to stay distant from my mom during the last few years of my mom's life. I believe she felt it was the best thing for her. Sometimes to keep a relationship healthy for you, it's best to stay away and that's okay too. Yes, it is perfectly fine to have distance in a relationship if that keeps it healthy for all. I have ironically had to do this too with my sister in return, keep her at a distance and that is why we now have a healthy relationship. I am not falling for the belief that I am to be close to my sister. Plus, I don't feel I need to be around someone that is hurtful and makes me feel like I'm not good enough. I will explain this more in the next chapter. I also know to send her light and love when I think of her. I'm not sure if Anne had that knowing to send light and love to people you care about when it's best for you to keep your relationship at a distance. This is key when maintaining a healthy relationship with someone you love but can't be around.

Mother and Son: I didn't experience the power and uniqueness of this type of relationship until I became like a mother to Brandon. I did not give birth to him and I didn't get him until he was 20 but I did everything a mother should do with a child with Brandon. I spent the time, taught him to drive, took him to his vocal lessons, took him to 300 gigs, shared my car with him, cell line, business cards, burned so many CDs and was honoured to go into the recording studio with him. Most of all, I listened to him. Many a time, I just stood by him and smiled, I showed him unconditional and constant love. Due to all of this, a mother and son bond was formed. I must say it's really hard to explain the strength and bond that we have or to explain the strength of the mother and son bond. It's the strongest platonic bond I have ever experienced.

This is another area that a lot of judgment has occurred. Shame on all those people who had judgment and thought we were in a romantic relationship. The dirty looks I received, the judgment for being after him for his money and the negative belief for being older than him. Does age matter? It has now been eight years and it doesn't matter anymore as Brandon and I just are able to be comfortable with this bond. We totally block out all the judgment towards the love we have together and our ability to show it in public.

I will touch on this topic right now. I believe there has been a false teaching or belief that love is not to be shown in public. I can understand that it's not appropriate to make out with a lover in public but it's alright to show love for your children, family and friends in public with a hug, a kiss or just holding hands. I also believe it's healthy to hold hands or share a kiss with your lover at any age and that it's a good thing to see love, as love is God, love is healthy and we as people should feel good when we see love. It is the programming of the masses that has made us a cold society. We are living in a cold society that shames holding hands or the showing of love and how did we ever get here?

This love between mother and son is also an unconditional love that must have some boundaries with it as we as mothers must always guide and teach. I understand it is hard with our boys and we must still teach them. Now it would take me a while to say things to Brandon. He would at times get mad at me and not talk to me for a couple of weeks. I would feel the lost without his connection but I always knew the power of love and the strength of our bond. He would at times try to be mad at me but that wouldn't last too long. I also found that he would be very stubborn at times when I told him what to do from my experience and when I was trying to help him grow he would do the opposite. I would be bewildered as I just told him not to do that and he is doing exactly that. I learned this quickly. Boys just like to learn everything their own way and the hard way. And still the bond and the love is the strongest I have encountered in my lifetime. There is just something very special about it. We as women and wives must understand this as this is one of the most important loves we have on earth. It's not a love to be jealous of and hopefully the women involved will respect each other. This is actually an area where jealousy can occur very easily, as the mother could experience jealousy towards the wife and the wife could also have a jealousy towards the mother. If so, this negative emotion of jealousy must be brought forward and talked about and dissolved, as it can cause a lot of damage. I did go through this with both of Brandon's girlfriends and it was very hard and how was I to explain it? I wasn't his birth mother and he didn't really like telling to many people what had happened to him in his lifetime. I'm extremely thankful that I can now say I have a healthy and loving relationship with Brandon's girlfriend, Lori. I love talking with her and spending time with her. We understand and value the importance of each other in Brandon's life and this is a wonderful place to be.

Abandonment from a mother, I think, is one of the toughest things to heal in anyone and no wonder. It is very rare and when it happens there is something that is not right to cause this type of abandonment as any abandonment is hard. One thing I know for a fact is that it's not the child's fault in any way shape or form and with the two situations that I personally know about, it was important for the child to understand this. Plus, it's just wrong to leave your children. It doesn't matter mother or father, it is completely wrong. If you have left a child, you must take responsibility for damaging the soul of that child and you must realise that you may have to ask for forgiveness from this child for the rest of your life. We are all connected but we are all on our own journeys and this is very important to understand after this unthinkable event has happened in a lifetime.

Now in both these situations, a replacement mother figure fell into place. I always say a prayer for the people that have the heart to raise and be there for someone else's child. These people are the healers of the children of the world. They have such heart and soul to come into the lives of these children and show them the love. Plus, to give tough love as the role of a mother is to love and to teach. Our children need to understand, respect and learn integrity to survive and achieve in the world we live in. These stand-in mothers or fathers need to also realise and encourage a relationship with these children and their birth parents. It's very important, even though it is very hard but these children need to heal this relationship. It may not happen until they are older but if it is possible then it is a great thing for everyone.

My mom and I had a great relationship but we did have a falling out when I was 45 and it was during a time I was learning to find my voice and my self-worth. I also had to deal with my mom always wanting to be present in my marriage. She just wanted to be with us all the time. I had to understand her fear of money and that was why she was so cheap with it. Next I had to come to terms with the fact my family was really the only family she had experienced and to understand why she always wanted to be with us. Then I had to let it go, as we had a strong love between us that needed to be there for both of us. I had to just accept her and her needs because I loved her dearly.

Our relationships with our moms can be from close and loving too distant and not so loving. It's the understanding that the love, that is missing, has to come from within and it is within. Therefore, if your relationship is not strong with your mother at this moment in time then that's okay too; accept it just the way it is. There are no rules or beliefs in any relationship and I will say this again and for any birth relationship, there is no golden rule that it is to be loving and active. Plus, this type of relationship will strengthen you and raise your level of consciousness which is why we are here in the first place. We have the love of God within; our souls are full of love and lie within each and every one of us. We are told this in the Lord's Prayer, Thine is the Kingdom the Power and the Glory forever and ever. We have the strength within to get through anything and any relationship.

Dad: My dad was a soft souled, loving man as well. He was kind; he loved people, had a shine about him and loved to be out and about with people. I believe I am very much like him. My dad had a good relationship with his mother, as we do know how very strong the bond is between mother and son. Therefore, my dad had love in his childhood. His dad was a firm man but loving as well. The thing with my dad was that he spent three years in a prisoner-of-war camp in Germany from the ages of 16-19. I know for a fact that war is created by the elite and therefore, the bankers are really the ones to look towards for such horrible things that have happen to us the people. Michael Jackson told us the truth in the song he wrote called, *THEY DON'T REALLY CARE ABOUT US.* War is just a means to create more control and to make money. World War 2 was created to keep the people down in strength and make money for the few families that are in charge and still are in charge of the world.

My dad never really talked about what happened to him and I do feel it greatly affected him and how could it not. He was locked up and in bad conditions during his teenage years. Now a days, kids at the age of 16 are snowboarding and enjoying watercrafts. My dad had three older sisters too, so he was for sure surrounded by women all his life and then three daughters. My dad also had a love for the United States, as he loved the people and the lifestyle. He started working there and spent quite a bit of time there when I was nine years of age. By the time I was 13, my mom asked me if I would miss my dad not being around and I said, "No, he isn't around much anyways." He had abandoned us as well. Something I still battle with. She then told me he was having an affair and that she couldn't stay married to him. I didn't understand it all at the time but I do now.

It wasn't until I was 16 that I saw my dad again and by this time, I really missed him, as I did love him so. He was living in California and he asked my mom and me to go visit. Not sure how that unfolded but my mom and I travelled to L.A. A place I now travel to too often. It didn't look like there was anyone in my dad's life; he had a nice apartment and my mom and I shared a room. Dad took us to the zoo, out for dinners and we had a wonderful week. I was glad to see him again. It wasn't until three years later that I saw him again as I travelled with a girlfriend to Arizona, as this is where he was living at the time. I did get to meet his girlfriend who did become his wife and she was thirty years younger. I know that there is judgment on age when people connect but I was happy for my dad. This is another belief system that is put into our minds or programmed into us. I don't believe love comes with a birth certificate attached to it.

My dad and my relationship was periodically weak, there was love but we just didn't know each other inside because we didn't spend time together. I probably could have used him in my teenage years but my first love parents were so wonderful to me that I did have parental guidance around. Like I said before, you usually receive the correct nurturing in life; it just comes in different forms and this is a new and good belief about relationships. It did take me a long time to settle down into a relationship and I wonder if I left these relationships first or gave my partner a reason to leave because I am so used to being alone and left without a male influence in my life. Do I push men away because my dad left me and I don't want to be left again, or do I just like being alone and without a strong male influence in my life? As I reread these last sentences, I feel that the words are truth, so I am going to have to go back and heal this and be aware of it in future relationships with men.

That is why the role of our parents is so important. We, as children, are so vulnerable and these beginning relationships with our mom and dad shape us for the rest of our lives. Yes, what takes place within the relationships with our parents shape us for all relationships to come. So if you need to do some healing with a parental relationship like apparently what I do, this is what to do. Go into a meditation and review what has happened with your parent and realise it was their journey to move to a different country or just not be there for you and it had nothing to do with you. Realise it was their past pain and what life had exposed to them that made them the way they were. It doesn't mean that this situation is going to repeat itself and have the awareness if you are in a new relationship that your behaviour could be due to some past pain from your parents and have the awareness for yourself when it pops up.

One other good question with our parents is do we pick a partner that is like our opposite parent? This statement meaning is for a woman to pick someone like her dad and for a man to pick someone like his mother. I have seen this often along my years of being a healer and working with people and I do believe I could be in this very situation right now which I will talk about later and for sure, my new love is just like my dad. ☺

Sisters: Well, this is a topic I can most certainly talk about from experience. As I said up above, I came into a family where I already had two older sisters, these sisters being 14 and 12 years older than me. I can remember as a child my eldest sister was softer than my middle sister and I really don't think they were too happy having another person to look after. My mom worked nights as a swimming instructor and they had to babysit me often. This must have been hard for them and one thing I know, it wasn't my fault. I can remember my one sister telling me this as if was my fault I was alive and she had to look after me. This belief she had was for sure not serving her or me very well at all.

I was closer to my older sister April and I still miss her to this day. There was a love between us which was nice to experience. It was a little different with my sister Anne. It's like we always had a block between us. We were opposite in nature and that could have had something to do with it. I realise now that it was her blocks that she developed as a child. They both were married by my 10th birthday and seemed happy in their marriages.

My relationship stayed the same with my sister April until the end of her life. I did dedicate my first book to her, *A Woman's Passage to Freedom*. I miss her still but she is in a better place.

My relationship remained tense with my sister Anne, even though I followed her and her family everywhere. Her, her partner and kids were the closest to a family that I had just like my mom was always following my family I was following my sisters family. She was a little old school and therefore, she was full of old, not well-serving beliefs. I also couldn't understand why she was so mean to me and why she didn't like me. I believe it was part of the fact that I had a different belief system than she did. In time, we had a complete break in our relationship and there was only distance. I finally realised I didn't need this type of relationship in my life and that I was better off on my own. This was a little tough, as at Thanksgiving, my mom and I were alone. No family at all, which is another belief that we as humans have done to each other. One holiday after another and I believe it is another money grab. My awareness is so acute in this area I find it hard to buy gifts at any time.

After a time apart, I heard from my sister and it was as if she had a shift. She actually started being nice to me and came to visit my mom and I. It could have been the realisation that our mom was declining in her health and it was good that I was her caregiver. She had let go of the jealousy and realised it was a fulltime job that I had taken on. I also

16

believe I understood to accept her the way she was and keep a bit of a distance between us. I had become much more conscious by this time and when that happens, everyone around you becomes more conscious as well.

I'm happy that in time, our relationship became healthy as a part-time relationship and this was just fine for both of us. Most of all now that my mom has passed, we seem to be developing a closer relationship. This, I am very thankful for, as now it's only my sister and I. Another year has passed and our relationship is still at a bit of a distance and when we are together, it is very loving and easy. I never thought I would say my relationship is easy with my sister Anne and it was. We have no judgment; therefore, we are living our lives the way we are to. Plus, she is very generous to me, as she knows I can use the help with a little extra abundance. I am thankful for this wonderful, loving relationship between my sister and me.

It is now November 5th, 2019, and my sister Anne passed away on October 16th, 2019. It was very difficult watching her pass and I miss her so. One thing I realised during this time is that none of it mattered. It didn't matter who got mom's rings or who spent time with who or what money was involved. It didn't matter at all once you are gone. We had all this unnecessary conflict over things that in the end, didn't matter. We should just live our lives in love, with no judgment and redo a belief system that is not working for us! We need a belief system that is created from the divine one from love and not the ego.

Brothers

I don't really have first-hand knowledge of this but I do have a few girlfriends with brothers, and I will pull from their personal experiences and what I know about men. My friend, Jen, has one older and one younger brother. She agrees that they both are a bit stubborn, like to learn on their own and have a few walls around them. This I agree with. She also explains her eldest brother is a bit colder and he is hard to get close to where her younger brother is much more loving and they have a close relationship. We do know that the eldest sibling consists of a belief system that really is not good at all. They believe they are to be the strongest, responsible for the siblings and the best because they are the eldest. This is a tough role to take on and one that could do damage throughout one's lifetime I also know of a woman that was the eldest and this belief did not work out very well for her during her lifetime.

One thing I know for sure is that we are all on our own journey, especially men. I have learned this so much with Brandon. He likes to be the one at the sail and the master of his sea! This message is from the Believer song, *Imagine Dragons.* It describes boys and men perfectly. Most of all, I have seen the cave man mentality still apparent within our men of today. This dysfunctional behaviour has been passed down for many, many years.

One other thing I know for a fact is that boys/men need lots of love. Like more than you think. They are also very loving and compassionate beings. Plus, the ones that are hardest to love need the love the most. Being non-judgmental with our boys is important and we must realise they are on their own journeys and we are just to love them.

Children

I will first start with my beautiful daughters. As they were growing up, I noticed my eldest daughter was a bit shy and that she needed extra time to communicate. Children at a young age need a large amount of attention and understanding of their own individual characterises and needs. We just can't put them into a box and expect them to be a certain way. We have to understand their differences, respect them but still be the parent.

My youngest daughter was a bit more outgoing but she didn't like to sleep. This was something new to me plus her not wanting to be alone, therefore I slept many a night on the floor beside her bed. Once again, I believe there are no golden rules and it's just trial and error that works with kids and your individual kids. Plus, it's also a good place to deprogram your belief systems and follow you heart and your intuition, as it's always correct If you have a feeling about what's best for your child go with it.

As my girls got older, they developed their own personalities (as they should); this was interesting and fascinating to watch. I also realised they were very different and had a unique personality which is the way it should be as we are all different. I did learn as a parent that I had to communicate with each of them differently. With my eldest, I knew she wasn't a morning person so I wouldn't talk to her too much in the morning. I would wait until she ate her piece of toast and we were half way to school, as I had to drive them both a distance to school every day. She also didn't like sandwiches or a packed lunch and I would give her $5 every day to buy her lunch. She didn't like to much talk around her and that was okay. That was just her makeup and I wasn't going to try and change her in anyway whatsoever. They great thing about Kate is and still is that she is my affectionate one. She still gives me the most wonderful hugs and kisses goodbye and she is now 27.

My other daughter and I talk a lot, as she is chatty; she loves people just like me and has an old soul within. I didn't have to be careful of her moods or energy which was nice but she didn't like me kissing her goodnight. She still is like that and I kiss her anyways.

Therefore, I knew as a mother not to put my kids into a box and I knew to let them have their individuality, as even in the school system, they judge and tell us how to be. I don't really understand where they got the idea that all kids are to sit still and be perfect little people. They still need to run and play outside and just be kids. These days, parents have much more to do as the schools are not providing enough activities for the kids. And now of course we have cell phones and Wi-Fi in the schools, which is damaging their cells and their little bodies.

We must remember as parents that our children just come through us. It's their lives and their journeys. We as parents are not to judge or use our unhealthy beliefs with our children.

Then we have the boys. With having a two-year-old boy live with me for a while, I can tell you first hand that the boys are different and so they should be. Plus, their energy is beautiful. They are busy, on the go and full of energy; what a gift this is. I would play ball in the house with Paul all the time and my mother would say no ball in the house. Well, this was my house and I would tell her ball was okay in this house. I would sit in the chair and Paul would be standing and chasing the ball; it was perfect for him and he loved it.

We try to put our boys in a box right from the beginning. We weaken our men and expect them to sit and be like girls. This is wrong from the very beginning. It is almost like they are grooming our children to be uniformed and in perfect order.

Recently, I was having a discussion with one of Brandon's buddies and he was rightfully expressing a lot of frustration with the way the world is today and he had a great take on the school system. Sam is around 30 years old, single and a father of three. He explained to me that he believes they are programming the kids to be in jail at a very young age. He explained: "The bell rings, you line up; you have to sit like perfect people and are governed by a principle." I was speechless because Sam had a very valid point and this was his perspective and that was totally his entitlement. Nowadays, kids are fighting back the jail-type environment at school. It's the teachers that are caught in the crossfire.

I believe we have to see the gifts in our men even when they are stubborn, as we know how stubborn they can be. Also, what I have learned about the men in my life is that the ones that are the hardest to love need it the most.

Now I have one other child-type person that is very important to me. This would be Paul's mother, Christine. Christine came into my life 13 years ago when she suffered a tremendous loss, which I was blessed to fill the void for. She's a beautiful old soul that I'm thankful for that always. It was a joy to have her and Paul live with me for a year during her time of need. I just supported her and loved her and this is exactly what she needed at that time of her life. We have experienced the most loving relationship, one with no judgment, no ego and therefore one of unconditional love.

It has also come to my awareness that it is more common than known that many parents are estranged from their children. This being a very difficult place to be and it happens often. In this situation there are no rules to follow just as there are no rules in relationships as they are all different. Therefore if you feel to be at a distance from you child that's fine and if you want to send them a loving message one a week or month than that is fine too. The only way of being that I would highly recommend is acting from you soul and not your ego. This being to send love, forgiveness and compassion.

Stepchildren

This is such a large topic right now as we have so many blended families at this time in history. I can speak on this topic first hand, as I have had two stepchildren in my life for a very long time. I did my best with my stepchildren. I treated them with love, part of the family and I was there for them. They were considered as children with no step involved as the good lord would want it to be. One thing I didn't realise enough was that it was hard for them being stepchildren. Hard for them to understand why their dad was in another family and that hurt them a lot, there was a hidden pain and, therefore, blame instead of acceptance was placed somewhere. Had I understood this more at the time, I would have had more family discussions or got them to a counsellor to help them through the shock of the breakup of their family. They were young and they just didn't understand that there is no blame. Blame is a manmade concept that doesn't serve us very well. Accepting what is becomes so vital in any situation at any age.

I also have the knowledge of another situation that the stepmother did not treat the stepchildren very well. She didn't cook for them, she would only buy for her own children and not for the stepchildren. She wouldn't do their laundry, she would send them out in bad weather when it was a snow day while their children would stay home. I really didn't think there could be such evil towards children but I was wrong, there can be.

Now these children went through hell until they left. They finally couldn't stand the mistreatment any longer. They found their own lives and families. I give these two children so much credit, as they have forgiven what happened to them and there is now love in these relationships. Really, all kids want is to be loved by their parents and stepparents.

Girlfriends

What would we do without girlfriends? I have been very blessed to have two very close girlfriends since I was ten years of age. They have stood by me always and forever and I have never had an argument with either of them or a disruption in our relationship. We can go months without talking to each other and the friendship and bond never changes. I must say over my lifetime these two relationships beside my children are my strongest, easiest and healthiest relationships I have experienced. There is never any judgment within our relationship and best of all there is only love. Real love, love from the heart and love that makes you feel awesome when you are around it.

I have also had a couple relationships with a few girlfriends that really didn't work out so well. There was jealousy and betrayal and a lack of respect within the relationship. Knowing what I know now, we were there to teach each other and to create growth within.

During these relationships I couldn't understand the lack of respect, as I wouldn't or couldn't betray another person. I still, to this day, have a problem with betrayal because of that, I have had trust issues that I have to be aware of. Also, I have a small circle of people I do trust because of this.

Then, of course, I found my voice a few years ago as I was pretty naïve for many years. I was even so naïve that I would even trust my ex with a girlfriend and you can image how that unfolded. I just don't understand why some friends want to have a relationship with your mate even when you are still married. And why is there so much jealousy? Like really, why can't we just be happy for other women and support them? Stand in their light so we become the light ourselves.

I also experienced a girlfriend telling me what to do all the time. I know and have learned that we are all on our on our own journey and these journeys are separate and that is complete judgment when a friend tells you what to do or that you should do something. I actually just went through this again, helped this woman out a lot and the closer we got, the more she wanted to control me. When the 'should' word came out again you can imagine how I reacted. Yup, not so good, I told her flatly,

"Don't tell me what to do, as it is my life." Now it's different if you are asking for their opinion. What I have learned is that everyone has the correct answer within and as a good and true friend, you could encourage your friend to find the answers within. You are the only one that really knows what is best for you.

Moreover, relationships have at to run their course and there may be more lessons for both involved to learn, As a girlfriend, you can listen, give support and pray for a girlfriend. Although if a situation with a girlfriend is affecting you as a person, it is time for distance within this relationship.

Men

It all started when I was six years old with my playmate neighbourhood friend, Jeff. Jeff was a kind and gentle soul and at this young age he became my best friend. We had a very special and unique relationship, which, as I look back on it, was an extraordinary relationship. We got along very well, never fought about anything and just enjoyed spending time together. Although I think it was more than that, we had a special connection, one of love and kindness. It was a connection from the soul. It was a sad day six years later that a 'For Sale' sign was posted on Jeff's house, as his family was moving to the United States. My family did visit once after the move and the connection or love was still there but that was the last time I ever saw him.

Ironically enough, the universe sent me another Jeff. Yes, he was very much the same essence of the first Jeff. Kind, caring, loving, faithful, supportive, great family, he was a wonderful guy. Our relationship also became my first sexual love relationship. This, therefore, brought more emotion and opened up an entire new can of worms. We, for sure, experienced jealousy, small arguments but we were able to maintain a committed relationship for five years. I truly wish I knew what I know now, as I would have married Jeff. By the time I was 20, this was what I knew about men. They were kind, respectful and loving human beings.

It was now time for me to travel and learn about the world. My sister Anne had moved to Calgary and it was time for me to follow. Even though she was hard on me, she was my family. I was travelling with a good friend, Jean. Jean and I both found employment in Banff. We were happy and enjoying the party life. It was at this time I met another man. We started into a relationship and things were a little different. This man was a bad boy type guy. He wasn't present in the relationship, he wasn't always kind and loving and there were always other women around. I couldn't understand why he was like that, as it wasn't what I was used too. The only problem was that I was in love with hm. I believed in him and I was sticking by my man.

Isn't that what we women do? Stand by your man? I stayed in this unhealthy relationship for four years and I believe this was a time for me to learn diversity. I, at this time, was learning about an unhealthy relationship and the emotions that come with it. I knew I had to get out so I started praying and my prayers were answered. My sister and the family were moving back to Ontario and I was going with them. I finally followed my inner knowing to get the heck out of that relationship. This was the time I learned that all men are not the same and some of them are not so nice.

My friend Jean had moved back a few months before me and she was working in a restaurant in Mississauga. I went to visit her and was hired immediately, as they were short-staffed. I was glad to be working to keep busy as the relationship I had been through was very dysfunctional and painful. I didn't even know you had to heal from the dysfunction of relationships. Where would mankind be if we knew we had to heal from dysfunction at a young age? If we only knew we had to heal from our parents, we as a society would be so much better off.

It was two months later that I had an unexpected encounter with another man. Jean and some friends from Banff had rented a chalet in Collingwood. We were there enjoying ourselves when the owner of the restaurant, I was working at, drove up to join us. I was asked if I had any idea why he was on his way to join us and my reply was, "NO." I must say I was very naïve as a young woman. My mother didn't teach me anything about relationships and, of course, we see the fairy-tale version of it and this being so far from the truth.

I was down in the washroom and then I heard someone and it was the owner of the restaurant I was working at and he started kissing me and I kissed him back. The only problem was that he was married and I knew his wife and children. I really had a hard time with this because of my values. I was young and didn't know any better at this time and the pull between us was very strong.

Long story short, we were married four years later and have two beautiful daughters. I became friends with his ex-wife as they were married young due to a child on the way and they truly didn't have any common interests. We started a good life together and we had open arms to his first two children. We had a lot of good times but the dysfunction that brought us together came back. It was something that I knew was happening but I did nothing about it. There was also something we all learned. My partner was a very negative person who liked to yell at me and the kids. I do know now that is exactly what his father did to him. History does repeat itself. We have to always look into the reason someone is acting the way that they are. There is always an underlining reason for someone's behaviour. Plus it can often be a learned behaviour.

Eighteen years later, we were in a dysfunctional, unhealthy relationship. I knew I had to get out to save myself and my future. I couldn't live in his belief system any longer and he was not willing to let go of what had been ingrained into him by his parents. Everything was no! I rented a house in town for me and my kids. I then started to read every inspirational book I could find and I was walking every day. I had experienced two difficult relationships back to back and I was in bad shape.

This was also the time all my relationships were dysfunctional. My marriage was a mess, my children didn't know who to believe, my stepchildren were on the side of their father, my neighbours believed it was my fault and that something was wrong with me. I was angry with my mom as she was around too much. My sister and I were not talking. When you live in dysfunction, you become dysfunction.

As I started to heal and focus on myself everything started to change in my life. Moreover, though the learnings of all the books I was reading, I started to raise my consciousness level. I firstly learned that mankind was very dysfunctional and that we had been passing this dysfunction to our children for many years. I had to understand why I had ended up where I was. Then I had to go back and heal my open wounds from my childhood as well. I had experienced abandonment and had some huge father issues to deal with. I learned that only you could make you happy, to be in service, to have faith and to let go.

This all took place over the next two years and then I wrote my first little inspirational book. I never thought I would write a book and one day, it just poured out of me. So be open to anything as anything is truly possible. This book being a very powerful read that has helped a lot of women.

I also learned forgiveness and that you forgive for you and to listen, to truly learn to listen. I started to eliminate the dysfunction in my life by controlling my thoughts and changing my beliefs and the dysfunction started to disappear from my relationships. Truly the key is to constantly work on you, This will change everyone around you.

My relationship started to improve with my children as I was present with them. I listened to them and was more peaceful with them. I forgave my mother for always wanting to be around me as I realised I was the only family she had experienced. I also forgave her and started to teach her to be more giving with her money. I just accepted her for her good qualities without focusing on the bad.

I also started to accept people just the way they were. My sister, I knew she had been through a lot as a child and that she learned to play the victim mode at a very young age and it just stayed like that. I loved her and I was just going to accept her the way she was from a distance. My stepdaughter wanted to be the woman of my partner's house, so I just gave it to her. She also wanted to be a mother to my children and so I just let her. Fighting her was not getting me anywhere so I just let her try. She, still to this day, is the woman of my ex-partner's house and I'm not sure how that works for them. They, for sure, have had many past lives together and I was just happy to be out of that. Now with my children, they saw through her needs and, to this day, have learned how to be in a healthy relationship with her. They just don't tell her much and they keep her happy. This works for them, therefore I have no judgment in concern with it. I also forgave the people that didn't know the truth and lived knowing the truth would come forward which it did. The neighbours learned the truth of my ex-partner and faded out of my life and new wonderful, conscious people came into my life. I had left the past behind and opened the door to the new.

Three Years Later!

There came a time that I finally ventured out into the relationship world or the relationship world found me. This was three years later. I started into a relationship that moved quite quickly, which was a lesson in its self. It was within the first week that I started to detect a shift in energy within me. It was something that I noticed but didn't want to pay attention too. As time passed, there was confirmation that things were changing and I started to pay attention. The question was. Was I willing to settle?

I met this guy at the bar and we had a connection. We had a first kiss and it was nice and I went home with him. Not something I would recommend for me again. He was a good man, hard worker but he was in a fight with his neighbours. He had a huge wall built between them and he didn't like to leave his house. I enjoyed being there but I wasn't willing to give up my life to always be at his place. After being at his house a lot, I asked him to my place over Christmas and it wasn't until the last moment that he said he would come. Then New Year came upon us and he wouldn't budge. My kids were here and I had plans and he wouldn't join us. I decided that would be the end of it. I wasn't going to take on this situation, as it wasn't mine and I wasn't going to settle for less than I wanted in a relationship. I knew that I wanted a healthy relationship, that one part consisted of being part of both our lives. We often settle just to be in a relationship and there was no way I was going down that route. I still, once in a while, think of him and pray that he was able to resolve his problems with his neighbours.

I next met a great man and things were going slower and this was much better. I was so thankful. He was successful, my age and a kind man. Our times together continued and all was good. To me he was perfect. Then things changed. I was a caregiver to my mom and my job was as a waitress in a family restaurant. He was looking for a more free and successful person. He did have the decency to tell me the truth and I was thankful for this even though it hurt a lot.

We, to this day, are still friends and he has been a great support for me always. Eventually I decided I had had enough of the relationship world and it was time to concentrate on my career and my loving duty to look after my 87-year-old mother.

What I Learned?

From what I have experienced over the last few months I believe and have come to the conclusion that we, as people of the world, have NOT figured out the relationship world. Yes, as I started into the world of dating, I experienced the same things as I did as a teenager. People are still playing people and I use the term people because for every situation, it can go both ways. It can be a man or a woman doing the same. This meaning it can be a man not wanting to commit and a woman doing the same but most common with men. Men are still looking for what they can gain in a relationship. I also believe women are more likely to be jealous than men. People are still judging everyone. I believe its fear that is everywhere and still running the storyline of our relationships and people are just afraid to just be themselves. There is not a lot of authenticity and this is needed for a relationship to survive in a healthy way.

My new perspective was that I was not willing to settle or accept the games of the ego in a relationship, as I was so happy living in peace and loving, finally just being able to be me. These are also times that you are actually finding you as a person and as an individual. So why do we fear it so much? Why are we so afraid to be alone? Moreover, why is being alone looked upon as being a bad thing?

I have also stated that most relationships come with dysfunction and it's this dysfunction we have been repeating for years and therefore, wouldn't it make total sense if we were alone for a while and out of the dysfunction of a relationship, we would actually experience personal growth? I think about my kids and how, at this very moment, both my girls are not in a romantic relationship and that I do hear amazing stories on how they are furthering their careers, personal growth and just being them.

Is it this fear that turns into control in a relationship? I look to this relationship where I see this exact thing happening right at this very moment. I wonder how that a person can stand to be controlled like that. I want to reach out and pull them the heck out but this could send them further in and that would be the worst thing ever. So I sit back and pray this relationship will take its course on its own and the right will come forward. We do know that control is completely from the ego and the more you control, the further your partner will go. It's also very abusive to want to control someone. From my experiences, staying in an abusive relationship is because of fear of being alone and a low self-worth. Self-love is one of the keys in any relationship.

I recently ran into one of the young women that worked for me at the Quarterdeck Restaurant in Victoria Harbour and she enlightened me with the most amazing statement. She said that all relationships have to run their course and that when you are in the relationship, you can't see the dysfunction. This statement I believe as truth. And at times you just want to ignore dysfunction is all around you.

Career

Besides the fact that there are many of us looking for and rebuilding a relationship at the age of fifty, there are also many of us looking for and rebuilding our career's at fifty too, this being me as well. Although I truly have to say that I have had to rebuild everything in my life at the age of fifty, yes absolutely everything. I would have to say the last two things that are on my list are my career and a romantic relationship and for some reason, I kept saying thank you for my man and my career in this particular order. This being because I like to thank God and/or the universe for things before I manifest them. After the last encounters in my life, I have now decided it's going to be the opposite, my career and then my man. I am very grateful for the lessons learned in concern with my time in the relationship mode but I'm happy to have realised that I need a solid strong relationship with me first. As we know, anything and everything takes time to develop and I'm thankful I discovered my love for writing and I have the vision to see my books on the New York number one bestseller list.

Most of all, I'm glad for the awareness that I need to build my career first. I now think to Oprah and her destiny of helping people, being in service and being a strong businesswoman. The correct people and the right man will come along that will embrace my career. Yes, this was a very important learning, as when I was flipping around with a new relationship that didn't really feel right, I was unable to be me with my writing and my purpose of helping mankind as a healer. Hoping when I meet the next guy, I maintain this awareness and put forth that I have a destiny and a strong purpose in life and that I am looking for stability in a relationship. Therefore, at this moment in my life, it's time to concentrate on my career and my writing, having faith that the right man will enter into my life at the right time. Moreover, I need to stay balanced as balance is another key in every relationship.

Culture

Does our culture govern our relationships? I would have to say a big "YES" to this question. Having a close co-worker who is from a European background, I learned a lot about the belief system that were inherited down. In her culture the man is in control, the woman looks after the kids, family and the house; the woman is silent most of the time. This particular culture has been handing down this way of life or belief system for many years. I know that now a day the youth involved in this culture are rebelling on all levels. This is from both male and female. The males no longer want to be the controlling ones with all the responsibility. They have the consciousness that a team is very productive and much heathier for all concerned. Of course being silenced within a relationship or family unit for the women is not working either. Women have more insight and intuitive skills that can be extremely beneficial in all relationships. One positive note is they have strong beliefs on no abuse and to stay married. They understand the importance of maintaining a family unit.

There are also some not so nice cultures that believe in total control from the man and allow abuse and lack of respect for women. We poor women have really been taking a lot from the men over the last 2,000 years. Look at how damaging this culture of belief system has been on the families and the children. Really, we must let go of the disserving beliefs that we have carried throughout time. We need to evolve more as human beings with the release of our cultural beliefs that have been carried forward. As I always say, a divine belief system is the answer.

In and Out

It seems to me that people seem to come in and out of our lives. I see this all around me and what it truly brings is sadness as someone just passed through my life and I miss her. I then thought to myself, well there is the saying that people come into your life for a reason, a season or a lifetime. This is a belief I agree with.

I then started to review the people that had come into my life for a reason. I thought of the kids that passed through my life and the reason of needing direction or mainly the need to understand why the world was the way it is. Yes, the first thing they always needed to know is why and I believed it's the dysfunction that we have just plainly carried from generation to generation. Interestingly, all the kids would understand this right away, as if they knew about the dysfunction all around them but just didn't have the understanding of it.

I had this one boy enter into my life for only a short time. He had been in great turmoil and through the path of the universe and his mother, I found him sitting across from me at my dining room table. He just really needed to know that it wasn't him that was the problem, that it really was the environment around him. Then it was how to maintain himself with the knowledge of judgment, blame, living in the story, being in a box all around him. I kept saying that it's good to focus on one awareness at a time and kept continually trying to end the conversation but this young man had many questions and so I just kept answering them. I could also see the very high level of intelligence, as he understood everything I was saying. This I do find with many of the people that sit and say, "I knew something wasn't right and thanks for the clarity." They also see more than living in the box or frankly question the negativity in the world and the dysfunctional behaviour. Most of the time, they are labelled that they have the problem but it's completely the other way around!

We next move on to the ones for a season which is causing joy and sadness, as it's when you get comfortable with someone in your life and then they are gone? I do think to this wonderful neighbour I had at the townhouse I bought in Middletown. She was the perfect example of someone that came into my life for a season and one that had lessons for both of us. When I first noticed her out my window, I would see her pushing a man around in a wheel chair and at first, I thought it was her partner; later, I learned it was her son. I can't, at this moment, remember her name. I do remember she was a wonderful, kind loving woman and I will call her Catherine, a name of strength. Catherine was always dress to the T, meaning elegant and refined. I, at this time, was at the lowest point of my life and trying to heal, so as time passed, she would comment that it was great that I was now wearing earrings on a daily basis and taking care of my appearance more during the growth of our relationship. We then started enjoying a cup of coffee and some wonderful snacks as she was from Germany and German women are the best cooks as per my friend, Rosy. This became a time of both of us giving each other strength, as this was the time of the passing of her son and she had already lost her partner. I can't really imagine the pain she was going through as the loss of a child would be a tremendous loss. Although I have lost Brandon so many times that I can, in a small way, understand the pain she was enduring. We spent many days having coffee and cake, rebuilding our lives and mirroring the strength we had within. I still have and cherish the beautiful set of pearls and earrings she gave me. I then chose to learn more lessons from my ex-partner and soon sold my townhouse.

It's now the two children that have come into my life for a lifetime that I seem to be experiencing turmoil about. These three people are, at this moment, at a distance in my life. Brandon, I should just plainly be used to it as him being in and out of my life or, as I refer to it as a roller coaster, has been more the constant for the past year. It's Christine and Paul that are now at a distance as well. Life has just unfolded that a break in our relationship has transpired. I know in my soul that we will always be in each other's life as I can see myself at Paul's high school graduation. I know that personal growth is happening for both of us and that our relationship is building strength. Therefore, all I can do is be in faith knowing that they will re-enter my life when the time is correct. I will continue on with my life being the best that I can be with my faith.

Relationships That Affect @ 50

Beside the many relationships that you are directly involved with, there are a few relationships that are not yours but these relationships indirectly affected your daily life and the energy that lies around you. Sisters' relationships are very open to be from one end of the spectrum to the other. My sister and I were so different, we lived our lives from different perspectives and this, after 50 years, has caused great strain on our relationship and all others around us. I think about my mom and how it affected her for most of her life. She was always trying to balance the two of us. This relationship affected my mom in a negative way for most of its duration.

My girls that I have given birth to are very close. I do know during their teenage years, there was a bit of tension between them. I give much credit to the easiness of Emily's character and her natural ability to ignore dysfunction and drama. They have also experienced me doing a lot of consciousness work. I always say, "Work on yourself and you will help everyone around you. When your consciousness level increases, everyone around you will also shift."

I'm thankful my girls have 95 percent of the time experienced a wonderful relationship between them and this reflects to all of us. It's good to have awareness that the relationships you are in do affect others. As being an outside person, it's all good to keep the drama and dysfunction at a distance because it's not yours.

As I reflect back to my mom, she did not deserve to receive the spill off of the relationships between her three children. Some may say it was a result of her upbringing of the three of us and still we are on our own journeys with the growth that we are set to experience. Just be aware of how your relationship affects others and try to keep your own stuff to yourself.

Holiday

I'm immensely excited about a holiday in Southern California with my two wonderful daughters. A small book enters into my existence at the beginning of my trip. I say to Kate, "Wow this is a great little book," and her reply is that she was given this little book called *Strengths Finder 2.0* by her employer and she's to read it. I immediately read the first chapter which grabs my attention and I explain to Kate the message in this chapter is when starting a conversation with someone, find the strength in people instead of the continual repeated obsession of talking about the shortcomings and the weakness of people. Kate smiles at me, listens and moves on with her packing for San Diego as we are on our way to the San Diego Airport to get Emily. I then say to Kate that I would like to bring this little book with me for our weekend trip to San Diego. Kate smiles and I place this little book in my purse.

It's a few days later and we are in the hotel room having a short rest as we have been, walking the beach, kayaking, eating out, and swimming in the pool, hot tubing, shopping, riding the roller coaster, going to the bar and listening to live entertainment and meeting great new friends. One of Kate's strengths is organising and doing it all when on vacation. I choose to pull out this little strength book and catch Emily up on the first chapter about the need for the world to focus on our strengths instead of the weaknesses of people. I then read the next chapter and relay to the girls how it states about the misconception of the line, "You can be whatever you want if you just try hard enough," and then the example of Michael Jordan, who was the best basketball player, but no matter how hard he tried, he could not be the same at baseball. I first thought, well he had a lot of fun trying and probably learned a lot but I am sure there was lots of frustration. I then close this little book.

We are now back at Kate's apartment in El Centro, she is at work and Emily is sleeping upstairs. I once again pick up this little book and the word 'talent' is now the awareness of the strength within, yes they are referring it to our strengths as being our natural talent within, nice very nice. They state it has nothing to do with formal education, degrees or skills, knowing that these are important, it's to focus on your natural talent within. This stops me for a second and I think to wow so very true and I reflect to myself as my natural talent as it has taken quite a few years to actually surface. I have the natural ability to write books with transferring insight to day-to-day activities and speak to the reader within the pages of my books. I also know that it took six years of practice once I was fortunate enough to discover my talent and I was able to work on it. Now be patient as this is a book on relationships and I do see already how this is all going to tie into our relationship realm. The book then moved forward into the different characteristics of humans and which type person you were and how to go into that direction for your career which all made sense. I found myself in quite a few of the given circumstances, one the communicator, the believer and most of all, the connecter which is the essence of bringing us all to one which I believe we need to in order to help our communities. There are professionals for success in working with people, counselling and teaching. This was a great little book and now let's transfers what was said to the relationships realm.

Starting at the beginning, a relationship must focus or be about bringing out one's strength, or as formally known as, he or she brings out the best in each other. I stayed in a marriage that completely shut down all my strengths as when I knew or had insight to anything that was out of the box or anything at all, it was always not valued or "you are wrong!" It was like being a caged animal. My relationship was actually sucking the life right out of me and I still stayed. I probably stayed until the girls were finished with high school, which I believe is a common place. I have also seen this same thing happening to a close situation where the woman is so controlling on the man that it has stopped his creativity as well. As time passed for me, I became able to break free from my marriage that was stifling my strengths and natural ability. This being the time I discovered my love for writing and my natural ability to channel insight into my writing. Knowing it was something I always had and something I am glad to have discovered even though I had to leave my home, family to develop it.

Next, if it's not working, stop trying so hard. Just like different jobs, some relationships are to be and others are not to be. Let go of the ones that aren't the correct fit for you.

Most of all, the last part of the book talks about a natural talent, a natural way from within. I believe our relationships are to be natural as well, relationships from the soul. These are the relationships that make it.

Therefore, I believe there should be no anger or holding onto relationships that don't serve us or are unhealthy, or ones in which one partner leaves, as obviously, it just wasn't working for one; therefore, it wasn't working for the other.

Twin Flame

Doors started to open for my book, *Just Being There*, thanks to my daughter being in California and the connections of her new boyfriend. I was in contact with a woman that was interested in writing a script/movie on this true inspirational story. I was ecstatic and had to acquire extreme patience, as this process was a slow one. I also continued to move forward with caregiving for my elderly mother, looking after all the kids in my life as Christine and Paul returned into my life and I was working part-time. I did have faith that something would happen with my love life, as it was not existent at this moment. I was all right with it but a lot of other people were not. I received a few comments that I should be involved with a man.

I had been in relationships since I was 14 and I was sexually active not that long after, so I felt it was just fine to be on a break from all of it. This could be another name for menopause, Men oh pause! I must say I did miss a sexual connection at times but I was waiting for the spark, you know that special connection when your entire body perks up and you actually want to kiss someone. Yes, that's what I was waiting for. There were men around; just not the right one.

So I went about my life. I was going out to restaurants, bars, listening to live music, keeping busy, walking, volunteering in my community and, of course, writing. It was easy to have a full life without a sexual relationship; there is always something to do and I never felt alone.

It was September 2015, when something happened to me that would change my life forever. A special girlfriend and I were out for lunch and it happened to be 9/11. As we were watching the TV screens, she suggested to me that I should do some research and learn what was really going on in the world. So I did. I went down the rabbit's hole and became obsessed with the history of mankind. Trust me, this was not a pleasant adventure and one I couldn't let go of. I spent every night for months on YouTube learning. As they say knowledge is freedom.

Next in May of 2016, I was given notice that my 90-year-old mother and I had to move. It was devastating news for both of us. As I thought to figure out a plan, I took into account that my mom was in very poor health and I was exhausted from being her caregiver. I chose to put her into a nursing home two weeks before my move was to take place. This being one of the hardest things I have ever done in my life. I got Mimi settled in and I rented the top of a house with three bedrooms. I was working fulltime, trying to visit Mimi and finding myself once again.

I found myself struggling to adjust as I hadn't been alone in years and now I was totally alone. I am therefore spending more time out. I find comfort visiting a girlfriend who works at a local restaurant/bar enjoying the people and the atmosphere. I guess when you own a bar for so many years, it stays in your blood, just like the TV show 'Cheers'. One time I take note of this younger man sitting in a chair over a few from me. He works in the kitchen of the restaurant and is also friends with my girlfriend. We talked a bit and when he looked over at me, I got this strange little feeling inside. I wasn't sure exactly what it was but it was something. He was a little rough looking but friendly, outgoing, a bit of a drinker and a bit younger than me. I looked at him, knowing that we were from very different worlds but there was something that was attracting me to him. It was a week later that I was sitting at the bar again and Andrew came out of the kitchen done with his shift and sat beside me. As I smiled at him, I strangely felt as if I had known this man for a very long time and that he had always been sitting beside me. The conversation was easy and I could talk to him like I had known him for a very long time, which, for me, was usual; it was a natural connection that I hadn't felt before. The ironic thing about Andrew was that he understood everything I was learning about that what was really going on in the world. At times, I would look over at him and look into his eyes and I could feel this amazing warmth flow through my body. He would smile back at me and I would smile too, thinking, wow, I didn't know this type of easiness existed.

It was a few days later that I found myself sitting back at the bar in the same spot, and lo and behold, there came Andrew out of the kitchen. He had jeans and a t-shirt on and he was a little heavy in weight. Andrew was dark-haired, clean-shaven with bushy eyebrows. He was also the head chef and kitchen manager. The restaurant was busy and the food was good; therefore, I knew he was doing a good job. As he sat down beside me, this connection and easiness returned.

The conversation this time started with Andrew explaining that he had seen me at an event of Brandon's that he was helping with, that he had asked who I was and that Brandon told him I didn't give birth to him but that I was like a mom to him. I was a little surprised as Brandon doesn't usually say that to many. I replied that that was true. Andrew then told me he had a daughter who was seven years old. I was thrilled that he had the joy of being a father. I looked over at him, knowing he was younger than me but I thought with his build that he was around 38. I knew he was way too young for me but I couldn't help feeling this strong connection to him. Moreover, he didn't drive a car or have a house or really anything and for some reason, that didn't matter to me. I also believed we met people for a reason and I couldn't really understand what that reason was or why God had put this younger man beside me to talk to when I really wasn't looking for it. I did know though that I needed someone to talk to as what I was discovering in the world was causing me some turmoil. It was actually quite a horrible experience learning what was going on in the world, it was like we the people are slaves and not too many people knew it. The worse part was it was right in our faces and as if they were laughing at us. They sure are happy knowing they have control and have us the people like zombies. Common sense when 1 percent of the population has all the money they also have all the control. It doesn't matter if it's the 1500s or back in Egypt, it's just a fact and that's the way the world is being run in the year 2016. Yes, right now. And the people just continued going through the motions being zombies with the bankers in control of everything. Plus, they are stealing our dreams. It's absolutely ridiculous what's happening. This actually saddened me so and I would say this to Andrew and he knew this as truth himself. I can remember him agreeing with me and me looking into his eyes and knowing he understood and knew that this was the truth of what was really happening. It was as if our souls connected as well and I didn't really know what was taking place. Everyone else I talked to about this thought I was crazy and that I had no idea what I was talking about, as I came back to the moment I just smiled at Andrew. The conversation would then change to something lighter and we would just hang out for the night.

As time passed, the pattern continued. I entered the bar and sat down and Andrew would exit the kitchen and sit down beside me. We would talk about the world as we were on the same page and it was nice and then our soul connection kicked in. I would look at him knowing he was way too young for me, as I knew there was an age difference but he didn't seem to mind either. He was just as excited to sit beside me as I was to sit beside him. I do look younger too and I am young at heart and I love to dance. People would look at us and I could feel they thought we were in a relationship but that was furthest from the truth. I also felt as if Andrew had been a bit older, we already would have hooked up as there was this unexplainable connection between us. It was a connection from the heart and soul.

There were also other men around and men that were more my age and probably, with society's opinion, better suited for me. The only problem I didn't feel like kissing any of them. It was like the closer they got, the further I wanted to get away from them. Also, the conversation was nowhere to the level of the amazing conversation that I was having with Andrew. Now this actually started to scare me. Was Andrew, this beautiful souled young man, the one for me?

I had been waiting a long time for a connection to happen with a man even though I had it for a bit with Mark but that was not meant to be, the timing wasn't correct. Then, of course, I did have a strong connection with my partner for 20 years. It did take a very long time to cut those cords from my soul to my ex-partners. It was a crazy experience as I would lie on my bed cutting the cords between my ex-partner and myself. Yes, good thing no one saw me gritting my teeth cutting those cords, they would have wondered what the heck I was doing. I must admit it was not easy and it had to be done. Thank God for Louise Hay's book, *How to Heal Your Life*, because it explained the soul connection I had with my ex-partner, so I at least understood what was happening to me. I'm sure he was also a past life connection, therefore it was even harder to disconnect this soul connection and we were not meant to be together in the rest of this lifetime. So now I am talking to God again, "Really God, you have sent me this young man that is from a different world than me and all I want to do is be close to him. What were you thinking? And are you sure?"

I kept going to the bar and Andrew kept sitting beside me. We would laugh together, have times of understanding with what I was learning, we were developing a great friendship. It was about eight months later that I felt this pull from our bodies like two magnets wanting to stick together. My entire body would tingle whenever Andrew sat beside me. I was still trying to fight this and sometimes I would just have to get up and leave. One time Andrew texted me and said, 'Where did you go? I had to go back in the kitchen to help cook an order and I came back and you were gone?' My reply was, 'I just felt I should go home.' The next time I was in the bar, there was a DJ playing and Andrew grabbed my waist and I actually pushed him away. My body didn't want to but my mind and my belief systems were leading the way. There was another time that we were sitting together and Andrew could smell my perfume and he turned to me and said, "What I could do to you?" and I replied, "That would never happen." I knew the age difference, but he didn't!

We are approaching Christmas and Brandon and his girlfriend have come to visit. This is wonderful for me as it is another relationship that has healed due to patience, understanding, letting go and time. We enjoy a wonderful time and the easiness of our relationship continues to grow. Although, my mom is not doing very well. This situation is a story for my *Taking Care of the Golden Years* book, I will say she is in bad shape and in a different nursing home.

Christmas has passed and I'm at work talking with a client about my mom being 91 and very ill. She tells me that her grandmother is 100 and is still living on her own. I then ask her what is her secret is? She tells me that she married someone 20 years younger. I must have had a telling look on my face that she then asked me if that meant something to me. I then said, "Well, I have this guy that has been sitting beside me for the last year that is younger than me and I have been keeping him at a distance." She then told me to stop battling my head and follow my heart and to go for it. I can still hear her voice and she was correct. I was battling my head and my beliefs over my heart.

It was two days later I was sitting at the bar with Andrew beside me and I turned to him and said, "Let's go home." Now Andrew had a look of surprise and we then both paid our bills. We headed out the front door and I walked towards a cab and he waited to see if I was really serious. I waved him over and we both got in the backseat of the cab. Next, we were in my kitchen talking, having a drink and Andrew kissed me. It was a kiss that sent something I had never felt all the way throughout my entire body. It wasn't long until we were in the bedroom getting into bed. At first, I was thinking this feeling is so different as if it was from the heart and I couldn't explain it. I woke up the next morning looking at Andrew sleeping beside me and it felt so right. It was the most beautiful moment.

The experience was amazing and all I could say to Andrew the next morning was, "Wow, I have never felt such intimacy before in my life." He just smiled at me. I knew it was different, special and a place that I hadn't been before in my life. I started to tell a few people about it and it was if I was stuck in time and had a glow about me that was easy to see. I couldn't even explain it as I didn't really know what was happening to me. It was a couple days later that Andrew was over again and it was even stronger of a connection and the same exact words came out of my mouth. "I have never felt such intimacy in my life." Most of all, here it was with someone I would have never in expected it would be. I could also see myself at work and my co-worker asking me what had happened to me. I had this glazed look on my face, amazing glow and it was as if I had been somewhere else; I really don't know how to explain it but it was something I had never felt before. My entire body was in a different zone.

I recently listened to a video on YouTube where this woman was describing what if felt like to experience intimacy over sex and the look on her face reminded me of me. It was the same and I knew exactly what she was talking about. She also explained that this feeling took place in the top of your body and not in the lower part. That it was a union of two souls and that it was the most powerful union and that it was the true definition of intimacy. I had to think for a moment on this one as I thought there was pleasure everywhere and there was something that had never happened to me before. Although all I had to do was look at her face as she was describing this intimacy and it was exactly the way I looked.

It was a few days later Andrew was back and things were the same. It was magical. I had a trip planned for January as my daughter was about to give birth to my granddaughter. I didn't want to leave my mom or Andrew but I had too. Three days upon my arrival to L.A., my beautiful granddaughter was born. It was a magnificent experience.

While I was away, Christine went to the bar and saw Andrew with another girl and warned me to stay away from him. As I returned, I was invited to a party that I knew Andrew was to be at and I wasn't going to go but in the end, I did. He explained that she was just a friend needing to keep other guys away from her. He was young and he was a little wild at that. I knew that though. The connection remained and he came home with me again and stayed for two days. During this time, I did get to know the deep dysfunction that was within Andrew. The hardships he had experienced as a young child from his father and from others. He said to me, "If I could change one thing, it would to have had support from my parents." I then learned that his present life was still totally dysfunctional. He was drinking too much and giving all his money back to his boss, the owner of the restaurant. The look on my face when I learned this told all and he realised he had to make a change. Over the next few weeks, we were always together and he was very supportive with the passing of my mom as she left us February 14, 2017. During this time, I also noticed that Andrew wasn't much for a committed relationship as he never really had been in one. He was definitely a free spirit. Maybe this is one of the things I loved about him and reminded me of my dad. Here I was being attracted to the same energy as my father that abandoned me. I also knew from my experience what was happening between us was special and rare. This did bring some turmoil between us and I wanted to hold onto this feeling forever and Andrew kept coming back but he never stayed long. I didn't deal with this well and Andrew would just block me out of his life when I became attached to him or acted a little controlling. I also noticed during these times that my high level of consciousness, that I had worked very hard to obtain, would at times fly right out the door. Yes, everything I knew at times left me when I was attached to Andrew.

During some of our times together, more was revealed and I learned Andrew was much more damaged from his childhood than I could have imagined. This didn't bother me at all as I am a healer and I can heal anyone. I also started to bring awareness to a better way of life for him which he was open too. It really truly was like we had known each other forever.

My birthday had just passed and I had a wonderful visit with my daughter and granddaughter. Things were going fine until a conversation took place between Andrew and I that would change everything. It was the conversation about our ages. Andrew asked me my age and I didn't answer. He then told me his age and all I could do was get up from the kitchen table and start washing some dishes. He told me he was 32. I was shocked as I thought he was older. I then told him I was 20 years older and he was shocked too, as he thought I was in my mid-forties. It would have been beautiful if we were only 10 years apart but that wasn't the reality. We were 20 years apart. We still had a beautiful night but there was a change in the morning. Andrew then stayed one more time and then he was gone. I was heartbroken and missed him immediately. It was like I was missing a part of me, a part of my soul. I knew what we had was special, one of a kind, rare, and I didn't want to lose it. I was a mess inside and it was very, very painful. My soul was in extreme pain, pain that I had never experienced before.

This then lead me to search out some answers. I had a psychic reading done first and was told he was a past life, that we had had many lifetimes together. Then I was on YouTube and I discovered information on twin flames. At this time, I had never heard of a twin flame. Andrew and I had all the qualities of a true twin flame relationship. I learned that our soul had been split into two at the beginning of time, one the feminine and the other the masculine, that we had reunited in this lifetime to help mankind and to show true love. I sat thinking about Andrew being the other part of my soul and that we had reunited to help mankind. I felt truth in this and this scared me too. I also learned that we were to heal each other and that it was our last lifetime on earth and we were to reunite. There was information about age differences too and it stated that it was common with twin flames to experience a large age difference. I felt some comfort in this but it didn't change the situation. I understood that the twin flame relationship would bring up unconsciousness in mankind and that our love and strength would heal them. They then talked about the difficulties with twin flames and their journey. I thought, oh great another true difficult challenge. I was hoping that maybe my challenges were complete in my lifetime but it looked as if I was due for my greatest challenge. Was this going to be my most difficult challenge?

Then it was explained about the 'Runner and Chaser'. This I totally understood and had a large moment of awareness as Andrew was the runner and I had become the chaser. He was running from the intimacy, his beliefs, commitment and love. Now me, I was chasing to get it back. He was the male and they do run from love and me being older and the woman who wanted to experience this love for the rest of my lifetime became the chaser. This was a position or situation that I had never been in before, I have never been a chaser of a relationship. You see I knew right away that this type of connection doesn't happen very often. The information was right there, Andrew and I were in a twin flame relationship.

This was difficult information and I became upset with God. How could he let me get into this situation with a man that I so connected with and loved that was firstly so damaged, had nothing and was 20 years younger than me? I had surrendered to God seven years ago, you lead, I follow and how could he let me be here? I was extremely confused and devastated. I then had a bit, just a bit of awareness that I was to change the old belief systems of the world so this could make sense and aren't we told the man should be older and there shouldn't be much of an age difference in relationships? Well, I had double whammies, there was 20 years difference and I, the woman, was older.

During all this time of unsettledness, I missed him so and my heart was aching. It was very, very painful. I then chased some more and Andrew ran more and then he blocked me. At first I was shocked that things had come to this and then I was a little thankful at this time as my consciousness was still in me and I knew to let go and have faith that if we were to be together, we would.

Soul Connections

We have soul groups, soul partners and soulmates. I do believe that we meet all of these people over and over again in our many lifetimes to create growth and to get us to remember what we are here for. During soul relationships we are also to clear karmic energy within these relationships. I started to understand this completely when I found myself a few years ago at a psychic in Barrie trying to understand why I felt like I had been in Brandon's life forever and why I was acting like his birth mother. To be quite honest, it truly scared the heck out of me. It was such a strong and natural feeling within but it made no sense to my head. There was no logical sense to this feeling. This is why I was asking for help. Now, at this time, I had already done a lot of inner work and therefore, my consciousness was strong because the more work you do, the more conscious you become and the more conscious you become, the more connected you become to your soul. This is a fact and something in the year 2017 we have lost, we have lost our connections with our souls and we are not paying attention to the power of the soul connection and that's why we are in such darkness within the world. Plus, people are selling their souls to the devil for fame and fortune.

I entered the room where Debra Johnson was sitting. She motioned for me to come forward and sit in the chair facing her. I did with a slight smile on my face. She said, "I have done your reading before?"

I said, "Yes, once before at your home."

She then looked at me and said, "So you found your son."

I looked at her in shock and she repeated the same sentence, "You found your son. You had lost him in a previous life at the age of six and you have found each other in this lifetime." Well, I must say that I almost fell off my chair, I had to pick my jaw up off of the floor and I was speechless all at the same time.

There was silence for a moment and when I finally was able to compose myself I said, "I think he found me." She didn't really care who found who, she just told me he would be like a son to me for the rest of this lifetime. The reading continued and next I found myself outside with the rest of the ladies who had already talked about their readings. It was now my turn to tell what Debra had said to me. I started off with saying that she explained that Brandon was a past life or a soul connection. I didn't say soulmate as he is not a soulmate and he is truly a soul partner and the room went silent and there were a lot of blank looks on their faces. I guess the topic of past lives or soul connections was something new to them. I then chose to change the subject about my daughter and that she was going to meet a new man when she took her next job. This man was going to be working on the same job but for another company. They all smiled at me as this was more in the scope of their belief systems.

This didn't really bother me to much as I had already lived fifty years as a healer with strange things happening to me that no one would understand, so this wasn't something new. Although I did feel that I was to research more about past lives as soon as possible. The answers came pretty quickly as my good friend and guide, Rhonda, at this time understood and gave me a book to read on soul connections and past lives.

It did become apparent that indeed Brandon was a past life and a soul partner. I also learned that soul mates, partners or twin flames will find a way to meet. Even if there is a large distance between them, they will find each other. At least I understood what was happening to me and why. Now I had to learn to balance this and not react in situations as much as mother bear to him. Long story short, to this very moment, I am able to balance a past life more and understand the dynamics. The best thing is that with Brandon's maturity, he understands our relationship more and is thankful for it. He did experience a lot of pain not having an active mother in his life. He now accepts me and I think he would wonder what was wrong with me if I didn't act like a real mother to him. Most of all, I do love him as a child of mine. There is no difference at all with the love I have for him and the children I gave birth too. Love from the soul is just as strong as love from birth.

Take the time to think about the soul groups that are in your life as well as the soul partners and soulmates? Or are you in a twin flame relationship? I think of Andrew, knowing he is my twin flame but he is nothing what I thought would happen to me. He drinks, he smokes, he swears but I can talk to him from the heart. I feel the most comfortable sitting beside him, more than I did with my ex-partner that I was involved with for twenty years. Andrew has no judgement, he is an old soul, he is smart, compassionate, kind and loving and isn't that what I asked for?

Settling

All the knowing goes out the door when there is LOVE.

So here I am writing this wonderful relationship book and my love life is all upside down. I have done the work with all my other relationships and they are healthy. I have written books on consciousness, healed many people and all that knowledge seems to go right out the door whenever I am in the same room as Andrew. It's crazy and I love loving again but really it's hard to balance all the knowing when your body just wants to be close to someone no matter what. I have already battled my heart with my head, with my head winning and that didn't really work out so good, therefore I don't think I am going to try that again.

I have this wonderful friend, Carol, who seems to be connected with me through the angels. Every time I need to hear something or need support, she is there. Sometimes it even freaks me out a bit. I was thanking her as she had posted something that I needed to hear in concern with my relationship that I somehow find myself in. I am also thinking I understand why people are single and don't want to be in a relationship. The difficulties with the twin flames would keep anyone wanting to be single, it's hard and painful. My heart hurts, I miss him and I don't feel at peace at all. So I decided to say to Carol I am in a bit of a relationship and I needed to hear that. She replies, 'Oh Jan!! How exciting!! I hope it's happy and healthy and caring, as you deserve all this and then some! I'm just thinking how lucky your "new friend" is to have you! <3☺' Well, that hits me like a ton of bricks because I don't feel my relationship is very healthy right now. I do feel the caring, love and intimacy and that's what has changed everything and I do agree I deserve it as all of us do. We all, as humans on this realm of a planet deserve happiness and love but we haven't figured it out yet. At least that's my opinion from my own personal experiences. Now I don't know if Andrew feels lucky to have me at all? Do we ever feel blessed to have someone that loves us in our lives? Right now I message him too much because I am a writer and he has some idea about my books and movies! I have given him a hard time. Ignored him once and not been so nice to him, so I'm not sure if he knows how lucky he is to have me. He is probably thinking the opposite right now and that's probably why he blocked me.

I, on the other hand, feel lucky to have him. I can tell him anything and everything and he doesn't judge me. I can be honest with him, I can share about my healing ability, my psychic ability, and my connection with God, all of it. Andrew is awake and knows what is going on in the world this being important. The sex and the intimacy is beautiful, therefore I do know how lucky I am to have him but really once again the age difference appears in my mind. Why is there a 20-year age difference? Andrew is lucky to have me but I am not sure if he knows that! I just reply, 'Awe, thanks Carol! <3.'

Here I am, this essence of love and I am feeling love for a man and once again all my knowledge and knowing is going out the door. I'm finding it a little unnerving but it's the truth. Andrew is gone right now and I truly have to work hard on believing in my faith and going about life as if everything is okay. Also knowing to stay in the now, therefore all I have learned is being put to the test.

And then there is more… Carol posts a tarot card which says, 'Leave a stressful situation behind. It should be easy'. Yes love should be easy and it's about furthest from easy right now. We just haven't figured out how to love and be loved, to receive and give love.

People just don't understand what love is all about or know how to love. We are here on earth to love, that's the entire reason why we are here and it seems for some and a large some of us that it's hard to love. I don't like to say things are hard but really we have to be honest. How do you teach someone to love after they have been so damaged? When they have never experience love, unconditional love and love from the soul.

I have always been an essence of love, I just came in that way and at times I feel like I'm out here all by myself. And now I have this person in my life that doesn't know how to love. First of all, this is so hard for me to even understand that our paths could even cross and that within a year, we could be in a physical relationship. Like really, how do things like this happen? Most of all, he is such a conscious guy but he has been through so much and now I am in love with him.

Jealousy

Jealousy has been around for a very long time! I believe this is because of the fact we have been living in the mind for a very long time. There wouldn't be any jealousy if we understood what a negative emotion it is and what harm it causes to everyone. Moreover, if we lived from our souls, there would be no jealousy. I'm human so I have felt jealousy at times in my life. I'm not sure if most of the time it was more like a feeling of disrespect, of envy or straight fear. What exactly is jealousy? Does it want something that belongs to someone else? Does it want someone else's partner or the love that is within two other people? Just saying it doesn't work that way. When two souls connect together, it's a special connection and bond. That bond does not get transferred when you switch up the partners. I have seen this so many times. Like your best friend, as you think she is your best friend at first, so happy to see you in a loving relationship and then all of a sudden things change and she starts getting jealous of the love you are experiencing and sharing with your partner. Sometimes the need for love and lack of love in their lives or fear of being alone may take over the rationalism of what is right or wrong. I have had this personally happened to me a few times during my journey and none of the girlfriend and my ex getting together in a new relationship has survived. I have also never been the other woman so I wouldn't even know how that feels at all. How can you betray a friend? Where is the sense of being happy for someone else and standing and supporting the love between two people and waiting for that to happen to you with the person you connect your soul with.

I remember when Oprah said that her girlfriend, Gail, was her best friend and how much she trusted her because there was never any jealousy; she was always standing with her in her light. When I heard this, I thought how beautiful that was and how blessed Oprah was to have a friend like Gail. Also, look at all the greatness that has come to Gail because she did have the consciousness to not be jealous of her girlfriend, to stay loyal to her and to stand in her light. This is very important people; standing in someone's light brings light to you. If we only understood this concept, we all would be standing in the light and there would be no wars, no killing and we would have a world full of harmony. We really need to be aware when we are being jealous. Whether it's with a girlfriend, a sister or a co-worker, or anyone at all, we have to be aware when we are jealous. We need to stop the unworthy pattern of jealousy and stop hurting the people we love. Jealousy also becomes an emotion our bodies become used to, then craves and becomes addicted to.

We create jealousy just to satisfy the bodies need to experience this emotion. Dr Joe Dispenza talks about this a lot. To change this, we have to be aware and control the mind not to create jealousy and to change the body's emotion not to want to feel this way, and if we understand this, there shouldn't be any jealousy happening. We have to break the addiction to jealousy.

I, right now, have this crazy situation happening again with my relationship with Andrew. It's like from the beginning one of my girlfriends has been jealous. She and Andrew have been close for a couple of years and she has been good to him. There has been talk about maybe a sexual encounter between them before our relationship started but it didn't unfold and I told Andrew, "If your relationship was to unfold that way, it already would have." The truth or the betrayal came when I was having doubt at the beginning and there was a push to get out of the relationship from my girlfriend. Should have seen the signs then but I didn't and I kept confiding in her. One thing I learned is to only confide in your family or friends that are not involved or connected within the relationship. You are just asking for bad energy if you do.

Where are we now? We are right smack in the middle of things, right in the thick of it. I believe Andrew is being pulled in two directions. Firstly, there is still the age difference and who would have thought that he would fall in love with an older woman, a woman 20 years older than him. Plus, he has never felt love and I believe he doesn't know what to do with it. Now a woman that he has cared for and has helped him all of a sudden wants him too and he doesn't know what to do or where to be. I'm just sitting back and letting life unfold. I do know with every essence of my heart that there is a huge soul connection with Andrew, a twin flame connection.

There also must be a past life connection. It's just too strong for it not to be. And if it's meant to be, it will be. I'm thankful for Andrew entering my life, as firstly, he helped me get through all my awareness of what is really going on in the world. It was wonderful having his support during these times and it was a difficult time for me and there he was always beside me with a kind soul, not judging me and knowing already everything I was telling him. As I look back on those times, I miss them.

It was wonderful just talking to him and right now, I haven't done that for a couple months. I really recommend talking to someone and getting to know them before you sleep with them. I know it's really the opposite these days but it's worth the wait. The intimacy and the connection was amazing because we had such a bond before we had sex together. And let me tell you if they are not willing to wait for you, then they are not the correct person for you. Let go! Have faith! And pay attention!

Will Love Prevail?

I am, of course, in the thick of it with writing this book as well and great awareness is happening. I went out to the bar the last two nights and no Andrew. He has worked every Thursday night for the last two years and he's not here. It just seems so strange without him and I miss him a lot. There is, of course, my friend that really is not my friend; yes, just tell a friend you love someone and they want them. I'm also becoming aware of the dark people who are trying to stop the love. There are also people who want the love to prevail. Yes, I would say it is about even with the people wanting love to prevail and it's with the people wanting it not to. I think to myself, has this been the test of time? Has there always been an underling battle of good vs evil or the darkness vs the light, or what it says on Andrew's Facebook page, **Legend says when two souls are meant to be together, the devil will find ways to keep them apart.**

Legend is the first word to look at. Legend means: a story coming down from the past that is believed to be true but cannot be proved to be true. I'm glad I had the knowing to look this up in the Webster's dictionary because it has shone light on the darkness. It is only a legend, so we can change this and this is exactly what we the people have to do. We have to realise that love is the key to everything and we have to honour it, respect it, cherish it and not let the darkness in. This means no cheating, no stabbing others in the back, no going after other people's mates, waiting for the love that is meant for you to show up in your life the way it will if you let it and when you have found love, stay with it, respect yourself and your partner. We are also told about this in the Bible that there is darkness and that the devil does exist and it's great to know we can change this.

I will get back to Andrew and my situation in a minute. Lisa and I were in the laundry mat as I was doing my laundry and she came in to talk to a couple friends she recognised. Lisa is a healer that is a good friend and is a big help when I need her. She was helping with moving some stuff out of a storage unit and I had to do my laundry. She immediately started up a conversation with a mother and daughter who were also doing their laundry. I was busy pulling my clothing out of the dryer and I heard the words, "My partner cheated on me and we broke up and I am now living in a different place close to town." I looked over at all of them and you could feel the pain in them. I just smiled and tried to send love and white light to them but my soul could feel the pain. It was spilling out everywhere. Lisa then introduced me to them and they were lovely people just going about life, doing the best they could with the circumstances that surrounded their lives. We had some small talk and Lisa and I left the building and jumped into my car.

Lisa started talking right away, saying how shocked she was to hear that news. This partner and wife team had met six years ago and had fallen instantly in love with each other. She said it was beautiful to watch as she was short and round and he was tall and thin. They then married six years later and it now was two years later and their marriage was over due to infidelity. Lisa then turned to me and said, "What is wrong with the men?"

I said, "There's a lot wrong with the men but as the women heal, they will heal the men." I did, at this time, have a flashback to my 20-year relationship as it was the same thing. I had my friends and neighbours sleeping with my partner and we had a beautiful family and we loved each other. That's probably why I could feel her pain so much. These situations do give validity to the quote above as darkness does go after the light but it's still only a legend so it can be changed. With all of society's influences, I do believe things are getting worse though and more reason to make a change. Just look at the higher level of transmitted diseases happening right now, it's out of control and that's God at work when we the people are off course, he lets us know the hard way. Therefore, in both these cases, the love did not prevail.

Back to Andrew, I could feel that it was almost split with the people being aware of the situation, half were the darkness not supporting the love and the other half were supporting the love and wanting Andrew and I to make it. Me, all I could feel was the emptiness in my heart without him. I missed him so much and I felt it really strange that this guy that sat beside me for an entire year until I took him home and let myself become vulnerable to him was nowhere to be found. I knew after that first night due to the most amazing intimacy that I was connected to him. I sent him a message through messenger and he was reading my messages but not responding. I just asked him to talk to me and tell me what was going on and make it simple. I, also due to all this stress over the last month, wasn't feeling good. I was fighting a cold and it was winning. I really could have just used the truth and I almost wanted to be set free from this situation, as it really wasn't serving me well but I tried that before and Andrew stayed in my heart. This is what a twin flame relationship is all about. There was no point trying that again as he would still be in my heart when I woke up in the morning. So I just told him I missed and loved him which was the truth anyways. He once again read the messages with no response. I wonder with the events we are going through, will love prevail? As soon as there is love, the darkness takes over and there are many a time that love does not prevail. Think about it, there is so much darkness in the world right now and the love is low and there are many soul connections not making it; we must make a change. I sit, at this moment, and wonder if the love will prevail between Andrew and me?

Frustration

I continued to go to the bar and be around the atmosphere I was accustomed to. Normally I would have accepted a lower level of consciousness or the only way to explain this was dysfunction or people living their lives from the ego and old belief patterns but something was changing in me. Watching Sue with Andrew I wondered maybe she was in love with him and didn't realise it herself? I think she saw the look on my face at times that was not anger or upsetting; it was "you have to be kidding me". Oh the games we play and the children we are, which is exactly what I said at the beginning. This is what I found when I got back into the dating scene after I had left my partner. We, the people, had not grown at all in the area of relationships. We needed to wake up to this understanding and our dysfunction of jealousy, fear of loss, fear of being alone and see the games we play.

Andrew next served dinner for his boys and Sue at the restaurant. He then asked for a new beer and placed it beside me as to say I am coming back but I had already made up my mind that I was going home alone as soon as the hockey game was over.

Andrew did return and this felt nice again, I really couldn't imagine sitting at the bar without him. It's also like he is my protector and I quite like it. The game ended and I had a few dances and said goodbye to him with a little rub on his chest, as I like the feel of his shirt that I got him. It is soft and cosy and then I left. I know when I touched him that there was a spark but I also knew I was to go home.

As I walked to my car, I thought about compassion for the people that are living in their egos. When I arrived home, I decided to write a bit more as my computer was working again. This was very healing for me and I was happy about my night as I had missed Andrew's friendship and I was glad to have had some time beside him once again.

My Mom's Celebration of Life!

I went around once from the airport arrivals and as I entered the second time, Emily was outside waiting. It was fantastic to see her and have her close by. There is nothing like having your children close to you. We talked, laughed and caught up on our lives that were now quite separate. In no time, we were moving quickly up the highway. Kate was not ready to meet us so it was decided that we would go to the lake house, which was my ex-partner's house and my house for 10 years, to pick up Kate and the baby. I was fine with going there because as time had passed, I had fallen out of love with my ex-partner and I had healed and let go of the past. Although I can't tell you how very hard it was to let go of the love of my family, but I knew that was not my destiny and that I had to move forward with my life.

I was greeted by my stepdaughter, who was not my biggest fan 10 years ago. She really didn't like me and blamed me for the life she had lost. Although things had shifted over the last 10 years and she was fine with me coming to pick up Kate. She was now basically the woman of the house and this was exactly what she wanted, so I give her credit for manifesting what she wanted even though my family was the sacrifice.

I asked Kate to drive as even though it had only been less than 24 hours since I had seen the baby, I had missed her. She was just an essence of light and I wanted to sit in the back beside her and soak up her light and love. It was also nice to have both my girls in the front seat as I loved them both very much and I missed them both very much. I had a copy of the service I had written for my mom's celebration of life and it was time to start reading it for practice and to get some feedback from my girls.

They just listened as I read it for the first time and I did tear up as I loved my mom a lot and it was hard talking about her. I was three quarters through and I couldn't talk because I was crying and it was at this moment, I noticed the girls looking at each other wondering if I was going to be all right. I then somehow finished reading it and the girls told me it was good and to practice a bit more. I was thankful for the confidence from them although I knew it needed some work and that I needed to go over it a few more times.

It was now the day of the Celebration of Life. Emily and I arrived at the Middletown legion and started to unload the car. We had so many picture boards that we needed to put down the backseats, therefore we only had seating for two and we had to leave Kate and the baby at home. Kate was not happy about her dress so Emily and I both knew she would be making a trip to Walmart and that would be all right. You have to be happy with the clothes you are wearing and it was an important day. Everything unfolded perfectly and we were all set up with a welcoming table and a games table of three bridge hands and a trivia question board ready for the people to arrive with a few minutes to spare. The picture boards were amazing and everyone enjoyed reminiscing and feeling the love of our dear Mimi.

Brandon arrived and started to unload his equipment and the people started to sit down for the service to start. I was very glad that my mom's secretary and one of her most valuable lifeguards were in attendance for the celebration. Mimi loved her job and the people she worked with in the swimming business. Brandon started off with a hymn from the shrine and this warmed everyone's spirits. I then began the service. It was going well except I had Emma and Isaac by my side. They are Christine's two youngest children, they were two and three. They weren't bothering me at all but the girls did say it was good that Christine moved them, as they were taking away the heart of my speech. I spoke as a minister and then did the eulogy and it went well. It was difficult for me as my mom was my closest friend and my longest relationship. I still wasn't sure how I was going to survive without her. It was then time for Brandon to perform Mimi's favourite song, *Harvest Moon*, and then for the girls to take over. My girls did an amazing job speaking and sharing their love for their beloved grandmother. I am sure she was watching from above and was extremely proud of them. They also talked about the bridge hands and the trivia question and then we had a small toast to Mimi. It was very special and a wonderful celebration of life. Next I returned to speak as a daughter. This was tough but it went well too. I also then felt the need on my mom's behalf to say goodbye for her to my sister Anne and to all her grandchildren that were in attendance. Relationships always need to be valued, respected and honoured. This was creating closure for all of them and this closure consisted of love.

Brandon then finished with *Hallelujah* by Leonard Cohen and this brought everyone to tears. He sang it so beautifully and he has the ability to cut into people's souls and this was happening to everyone. Even one of my good friends had to come from the back of the room to sit beside me and I was then comforting her. She had lost her father a few months before and had not experienced closure; therefore a lot of her emotions were coming to the surface. This will happen when we don't feel what we are to feel. Our emotions stay in our subconscious and within the cells of our bodies and when a trigger takes place, these emotions come forward and this then takes over and is running the show. This is why it's important to feel what you are feeling, to be aware of your emotions and to let go and free the cells of our body.

Lunch was served, Brandon continued to play and the people stared to mingle. It turned out perfectly and I was very thankful. I said my goodbyes to all the visitors and it was Kate and baby, Emily, Brandon and I left in the hall. The girls did such a great job and it was nice having Brandon here to help pack up. Brandon went and pulled up my car for me and helped load everything. He is such a kind, loving, respectful young man and I'm thankful to have him in my life. We all then headed up to Boston Pizza which was Mimi's favourite place to go and also where Brandon's lovely girlfriend, Lori, worked. She was unable to attend as it was an important shift for her to work. We had a bit of a rocky start in our relationship and that is okay. As I said before in the beginning of the book, relationships come in different forms. Brandon and I have a strong mother and son bond as we spent the time together and I did what a mother would do for her children with Brandon. Lori understands this now and we all get along well and have a special love and respect for each other which is just beautiful to experience. It's like she is becoming another daughter to me and this is very special.

We are all enjoying a magical moment as I have my three children with me and my very beautiful and special granddaughter. We are having a great time and Brandon heads out for a smoke and all of a sudden there is this man standing at our table. I know him from the place that Andrew works and he has seen Andrew and me together. As I look at him, I notice he has a distressed look upon his face. He then says to me, "Andrew is a mess. Did you see the post he made on Facebook? He was drunk and it was disgusting and I don't know what is wrong with this guy." The first thing that pops into my head was, really God you are only going to give me two hours break after just saying goodbye to my mom?

I said to him, "No I didn't see it and I haven't seen him lately." He then continued to talk about Andrew and not in such a nice way at all. I was surprised as I had seen him on Thursday and he looked good and everyone was telling me how great he was doing. This man also questioned both Kate and Emily asking them if they knew Andrew. They both replied. "Yes." He then asked what we were doing as we were dressed up and I didn't feel it was in any way any of his business and I didn't answer. He then told me I had beautiful girls and left the table. Emily said, "That was really strange, Mom." I agreed and right at that moment, Brandon returned to the table. I'm not sure if he could notice the change in energy but I was having a hard time keeping it together. Andrew was still in my heart and I was missing him today. The only problem at this time was that I was tired and therefore, I went to fear that maybe there was something wrong with Andrew and all I could do was think about him. All I really wanted to do was save him! We finished our time at Boston Pizza. It was a wonderful time and it was great to have Lori part of the ending of the Celebration of Life for Mimi!

The girls dropped me off as they were going to the lake to see their dad and I knew that I was going directly to bed as I was exhausted. As I lay in bed, all I could think about was Andrew. Firstly, I thought, well you were given exactly what you asked for, as I didn't say anything about age or him being successful; all I wanted was someone I was in love with that was kind, loving, an old soul and a conscious man. Although Andrew knew nothing about love and when you walk away from it, you fall apart but then I thought that he did experience love, even with the age difference, it was true love, real love and I know and believe in the power of love. I then sent Sue a text saying I heard that Andrew was in trouble and that's what happens when you don't follow what God gives you that you have asked for and that maybe, just maybe she could help him out and send him in the correct direction. Then I passed out for the next three hours. I did wake up thinking I probably shouldn't have sent the text but I was worried about him so at least I knew she would check on him.

It was the next day and I felt the need to reach out and check on Andrew. I reached out and contacted Brenda, another employee at the location that Andrew worked at and I had become friends. I was doing a bit of healing on her and she was very close with Andrew and I was thankful that she was in his life. Brenda's first reply was that guy is always talking about other people behind their backs and he never tells the truth. I thought, are you sure? And then I asked her if she could check on Andrew and let him know that I wanted to talk to him. I just wanted to talk to him. Brenda told me she would tell him when she next saw him. Monday was a holiday and the restaurant was closed. I felt good about it at least there was someone I could trust and someone that cared about Andrew from the heart and didn't influence him to affect her life. This is a huge subconscious trait that at times we are not even aware of and a favourite game of the ego. Like Sue probably doesn't even know that she is influencing Andrew for what is best for her. He is her friend and companion and she does not want to be alone even if holding onto him is the best for her and not for him.

It was Tuesday and I had to go to the bank and I saw Andrew having a smoke outside the side of the restaurant and he looked fine and happy. I think he was wondering what was wrong with me as when our eyes met there was no smile on my face. I was upset about something; it also seemed like he was a little surprised and then I continued to the bank. A few hours later, I text Brenda saying I saw Andrew and he looked fine. She replied that she had told him that I wanted to talk to him and that he hadn't responded. I thanked her and was happy that at least he knew I cared and wanted to talk to him. There is nothing like your heart hurting for someone you care about and the worse things is not being able to talk to them. This, for sure, was a new place for me and I was getting used to it but it wasn't an easy spot to be in, especially because I like to talk and text. I do realise that Andrew was teaching me to be strong and making me deal with non-attachment. He was creating growth for me. This is one of the main purposes with twin flames; they are to create growth within themselves. Andrew had to be growing too. That's just how it works. I thanked Brenda for helping and we just left it like that.

It was now Thursday and I had to work late but I knew I had to go to the bar to talk to Andrew. I just felt like I needed to talk to him. Brandon was playing but he started early and said he would most likely be finished before I got there. The hockey game was on and this was another reason I was going and I was thankful for this. Andrew knew I liked to watch the hockey and I liked to watch it with him. I got home showered and headed to the bar. I was walking towards the front door and turned the corner and there was Andrew standing there and he had on the other shirt that I had bought him. The first words out of my mouth were "perfect timing" and he smiled at me. I then said, "I have to talk to you." Andrew then started talking to me explaining he heard about what had happened.

He said, "I'm not very happy about it and this guy is always saying bad things about me for no reasons." I relayed to Andrew that all I said to this guy was that I hadn't seen you. Andrew then showed me the post and it was nothing at all. We then entered the bar.

Brandon was standing at the front door as he had just finished playing. He was talking to a couple customers. I just stood to the side for a second and he came over and gave me a hug. I then took a seat at the bar to watch the hockey game and I noticed before I sat down that Andrew's sweater was on a chair and he had a beer on the go. I thought this was strange as he usually worked until 10 but this was a different week with the holiday on Monday. I then sat down beside his chair. Brandon then came over and asked me how my day had been. He is such a good boy, kind and respectful. We had some small talk and he then started to pack up his equipment. Andrew then sat down beside me and so I turned to him and said, "So you are good?"

He replied, "Yes I am and really this is the best I have felt in my entire life." I just smiled at him as knowing someone you love, have cared for is doing well, warmed my heart. I was happy that he was happy and I do believe I had something to do with that because I loved him a lot. The last time he was over I told him that I loved him and he said to me, "I know you do." He knew in his heart that he was truly loved and that made me happy.

Brandon then said goodbye to both Andrew and me. I could detect a little strangeness with Brandon as I believed we were all from the same soul group and the three of us had been in a few past lives together.

Brandon left and we were enjoying the hockey game and then a feeling of upset, or I would have to say being pissed off, came up in my atmosphere. I then turned to Andrew and said, "I am really pissed at this guy and he really has a problem."

Andrew agreed and said, "I feel like saying something to him as it was my character he had attacked."

I said, "Well, the timing wasn't good and he really upset me and that day was special for me; it was the celebration of life for my mom." I was wondering to myself, at this moment, where my angels were as I know I am extremely protected. I then picked up my phone and texted Brenda saying what a jerk this guy was. She responded right away saying, 'yes, I have wanted to say something to him many a time but I can't because he spends a lot of money in the bar and she is not the owner, therefore she has to say nothing.' One rule we had at the restaurant I owned was you see nothing, you know nothing and you say nothing. As an owner, I probably would have told this customer off as I never have put money over people and right now my righteousness part of my essence was strong and I probably would have to say something. The line, "Didn't your mother teach you, if you don't have anything nice to say, don't say anything at all." Brenda agreed that the timing wasn't good with it being the day I said goodbye to my mother. I did tell Brenda that I would one day soon have some choice words for this man. I know that the correct time would show itself and the correct words would come forward too.

I then went back to knowing what I know and understanding the dysfunction of the world and this individual man. Maybe this was the only way he knew how to get attention? Maybe he developed this pattern when he was a small child and he, as a man in his late 50s, was still holding onto this behaviour pattern. Moreover, did he want to create the emotion that came along with it? For him and the people he was affecting? Compassion for this man was what came forth next for me. It was sad that he was unable to break the patterns of his ego. That he had to live in a life like that. I knew to pray for him for his awakening as no matter what stage he is in life, there is always hope.

I then took myself back to the now with enjoying talking and sitting beside Andrew. I really missed just being his friend. We were both healing just being beside each other again. The game was good and Andrew's team was winning. There was still a Canadian team involved but Andrew had a favourite and this was going well. The game then, all of a sudden, tied up and we were into overtime. Then the next thing I knew, Sue came into the bar, as she was working the late short shift on the bar. It was quiet in the bar. She then grabbed the schedule and sat down in Andrews's chair. I was a little taken back as she never acknowledged me or said a word to me. It was the strangest feeling and it was like being back in high school. I actually started to think this was a little funny. Then I almost started to get the laughs and I had to lock in my emotions. Andrew stood on the other side of her when he returned as he wouldn't have fit between us and said, "Hello." Sue was like family to him and they were close. I was just minding my own business and letting things unfold. The next thing Andrew did was he went and got her a chair and moved her over and sat back down in his spot. I looked over at her and she was not happy. I really couldn't believe such childish behaviour and I had to have compassion as something else was running the show with her. It could have also been the owner not wanting Andrew and me sitting together at the bar. She was his go-to person when he wanted control of something going on in the bar. She was talking to him a lot and then his team scored and we all cheered together. Andrew did have a shine about him that he had never had before and it was beautiful to see. It was like a light was shining from his soul. He had a new strength from within. I then paid my bill and started to get ready to leave. Andrew looked over at me and I said to him, "You are sure you are good?" He nodded his head up and down with a warm smile on his face. I then said goodbye and left the bar. I felt peace on my way home as I was glad he was doing well. I still missed him but I was glad he was good.

It was sad saying good-bye to my three girls. I was extremely proud of them as they had done a fantastic job on the Celebration of Life for their beloved grandmother, Mimi! I had some healing to do and to rest for a few days. I did have the excitement of Brandon's boat trip ahead of me; I was writing a lot and working on my career. I knew to make it about Brandon this week and this was exactly what I was going to do. I wasn't sure who was going on the boat trip. I didn't really care because I was staying in faith and this was the only way I was going to live at any moment in my life. It did say on the list on the internet that Andrew was going to attend and I was hoping that he would. It would be nice if he became more a part of my life and Brandon, as this will always be a big part of my life.

Back To Work!

I had to work the next three days so I was only going to be able to work and sleep for the next few days. It was now Wednesday and I was close to making it through my three days. I believe in the PEMF therapy and was thankful for the healing frequencies and this job. I had worked till close the night before and I was counting down the hours until I was finished my shift. It was pretty quiet and then all of a sudden, the door opened and one of our regular customers came into the clinic.

Jennifer was a regular customer for the last few years and she was a great person. She entered the clinic and sat down close to me. She told me she was waiting for her homeopathic doctor and her partner. I looked a little surprised as she didn't have an appointment. Jennifer picked up on this and said, "My partner and I are thinking of purchasing a unit for home use and my doctor is going to see which unit we resonate with."

I said, "That's great and yes some people resonate better with different units."

They arrived just after our conversation and got right to work with doing muscle testing and testing the different units out. I was just watching and paying attention. Jennifer and I had a respectful relationship as a customer and employee, so I was having faith that all would go well. Her homeopathic doctor, Rob, seemed very knowledgeable and gifted too. Gifted in the same way I was as a healer and this was nice to see. I was picking up on his psychic abilities as well and I was not too sure if he felt comfortable with this. He was watching me quite closely while working at the task at hand.

Then one of the new owners of the clinic walked it. I was a little nervous on how she would react, as I wasn't sure if these people were crossing any boundaries of integrity for the business. I had a pretty good relationship with all three of the new owners but I didn't see them much. They all had different businesses outside and only worked small hours in the clinic. There were also some things happening within the business that were boarder line with conflicts of my belief system and I still knew I had to be there for some reason. I also needed the job and they needed me so we were all just hanging in there, knowing there was some strength happening for both of us.

My boss seemed to have confidence in me that what was taking place in the clinic at this moment was okay. I was thankful for this as I wouldn't do anything to hurt anyone or hurt the clinic in anyway. I introduced and included her in what was taking place and she seemed happy about that and pleased that I was looking after this situation. We all moved to another room and we chatted a bit to the side and then she said, "Jan, you have this under control," and then left the office. This was nice to hear as it doesn't matter what age or what type of situation, it is good to know your employer has confidence in you.

I then returned to the conversation and to the mussel testing that was taking place. I found it quite interesting and I also found Rob quite interesting. He looked just like an average man in his early 50s. I believe he was a healer as well. I was just standing off to the side and he said to me, "You have something above your head could you please come into the middle of the room."

Relationships can start in many different ways and even though I just met this man, we were starting or developing a relationship. I now had to decide whether or not I was going to participate and trust this person. I listened to my instinct and moved into the middle of the room. He then asked me to put out my right arm and then started doing some mussel testing by moving my right arm to my head and above my head. He first said to me, "Your destiny is about to unfold."

I smiled at him and said, "Yes, it is." He then explained he was continuing to test my energy and that he didn't come across this very often. He then said, "You are connected to your higher self and that's what I could see above your head." He then said again, "I don't see this very often."

I said, "Yes, you are correct, I am connected to my higher self and I have worked very hard to get here." I could see him looking all around my head and seeing things above my head. I said to him, "Do you see all the angels around me?"

There was silence or a moment and then he said, "You have to heal your heart chakra. You have been carrying around a lot pain in your heart."

Now there was silence from my end as I knew he was correct. I said, "Yes, I do." I thought to myself was he detecting the twin flame connection and the fact that my soul had found the other half of my soul and we were in the separation stage right now or had my heart been broken for a long time? I was doing okay but my heart and soul was missing Andrew. The conversation then ended with Rob saying, "I have never encountered this before." He then walked out of the room and left the clinic.

I was stunned and I turned and looked to Jennifer and her partner. There was silence for a moment as we all were taken back on what had just happened. I then told her that my destiny was with my writing career and that I was a healer. I then explained that I don't tell too many people that I am a healer and that Rob was correct with what he had said. She just smiled at me and said, "He is a very interesting man." She and her partner thanked me for my time and left the clinic. I then sat quietly for a moment, knowing my heart was talking to me again. I knew it still needed healing and I then started thinking about Andrew. Was the relationship with him a relationship to learn from or was it a relationship to heal from, or was it both? I also knew for some reason that it was a past life healing. Not quite sure how to explain that but I knew for sure it was a past life healing. I was hoping for this healing to take place soon.

I also was impressed that during all the work I had done over the last 10 years I was able to raise my consciousness level and connect with my higher self. This was a gift that came from this encounter with Rob. I had released the ego and was connected and living from my higher self and my soul. It took a lot of work and dedication and I was thankful for this.

Then Brandon came into my awareness, as once he told me to heal my heart in a song he wrote about me three years ago. I listened to his words in this song and I had done everything I could to heal it. I had done the work and I guess I still needed to do more work and heal more of my heart.

Next it was raining men, they were everywhere and of all ages but I still woke up and went to bed with Andrew in my heart. I wasn't going to ignore that and just go with someone else. I still had the issue that if I didn't want to kiss another man and there was no point going any further. I did have an amazing healing with Andrew but it didn't last and we were on a separation time and it was painful. I still can remember the intimacy, as it was so amazing and healing. But now he was gone and all I did was miss him. I knew this was my last area of healing and I was totally living in faith with this situation. I was so ready to love again; it just had to be with someone I had a connection with. I still couldn't understand why it was with Andrew but it was with Andrew, it just never changed. I would talk to God often about it and I wished the age difference was not as much. I was trying and getting close to the feeling that age didn't matter at all. Although, I was still programmed like everyone else was that age was a factor in love when really it had nothing to do with it.. I could see Andrew and myself together and you not being able to tell the difference in our ages when he was 60 and I was 80. Most of all, I could see us leaving this lifetime together and that being all right for both of us. So as the men came, I just acted as friends which they all were and kept my distance from them.

Brandon's Boat Cruise

It was now time to get ready for the next event which was Brandon's annual boat cruise. This would be the 5th cruise I had attended and things were fabulous this time around. Yes, over the last five years, there had been, of course, ups and downs in our relationships and this was okay. Actually last year, I had to ask permission to see if I was welcome at this boat cruise as they were both upset with me. I look back and laugh a bit as we have all grown so much since then, therefore there has been lots of lessons and lots of growth. Most of all, there is always hope and always room for change in any relationship.

This year, I was welcome to make a couple veggie trays and to board the boat early. Most of all, I was able to be close to Lori and this really was special for me. I was starting to look at her and feel more and more she was like another daughter. This warmed my heart so much and I knew it made Brandon extremely happy.

It was the night before and all was good and I received a reminder that I was to volunteer at the MCC Centre in Middletown for a fundraiser for the rotary club. I was to do readings for the evening which I was happy to do. I was thankful they had sent out a reminder and that I was off on this Thursday as I usually worked every Thursday. I thanked God for the assistance on this evening working out with the timing. I arrived and knew where to set up, knowing the correct women would be seated across from me to have the guidance and direction given. I was using my tarot blocks and they are guided by the angels and also knowing I have a direct line to God.

The night started off great with an amazing down-to-earth extremely smart woman that was already on a spiritual path and needed some conformation on her journey. **I love knowing that every time you meet someone new, it is the starting of a new relationship, new relationships being one of the most amazing things to unfold in our lives**. She had a beautiful soul and I was thankful having been sent to appear on her path. I do believe that we are to meet everyone we do and that they have a message or are to be in our lives for a short or long time.

The night continued with beautiful women sitting across from me, learning from their evening and having fun too. I was a bit tired after this event as it is always a bit challenging having multiple readings in one evening. I then wanted to have a beer and get some take-out. I really did enjoy the food that Andrew made and felt the love when he made me a salad so I walked to the restaurant. As I entered the front doors, there was Andrew and one of the new great bartenders. John immediately asked if I would like a Corona and of course I said, "Yes, please."

Andrew then said, "And a tequila!" I thought how cute he is taking a little bit of ownership and I thought maybe he was a little jealous. I took off my coat and went to the bathroom with a smile on my face. I thought to myself that the connection was still there, it's always still there.

I then returned. Andrew hung out for a minute and I told him I had just done eight readings and he smiled at me. One of the greatest things was that I could tell Andrew anything. There was never any judgement and even when we took it to the next step, he was supportive of it. He totally understood I was a healer and this was such a gift to me. He then returned to the kitchen. John and I talked for a bit and this was nice. John and I realised we had something in common; we had both been stung by Marilyn. She is someone mentioned in my *Just Being There* series book number II. She was his aunt and he was a little upset that a family member could treat another family member in such a bad way. I explained she was living from her ego and the ego doesn't understand family or make any concessions for family members. I then ordered my salad and was happy to have some greens coming my way and it was nice to know Andrew was making them. I ordered another beer and placed my credit card out to pay; I was tired and needed to go home. Andrew did finish work and was talking with some of the other staff when I headed out the door with my salad in hand. I wondered as I left if he was still planning to attend on the boat. I knew whatever way it unfolded, it would be perfect.

I got up the next morning, got dressed and went to get the veggies for my trays. I was excited to be a part of this wonderful boat cruise of Brandon's and I was very proud of him. That feeling when your child is doing great and living the life they deserve is such a beautiful feeling. It took me about an hour to cut all the veggies up and then make the trays. The weather was still a bit cool and it was okay for jeans and a nice shirt. I arrived at the boat just after five as Brandon said they would be there early and, of course, he was not there when I arrived. Lori actually arrived first so I headed over and she was so great to me: gave me a big hug and said she was happy to see me. She offered to help me get my trays and I said it would be okay and I would get them. We then with the help of some of her lovely girlfriends, set up the food on a large table. Lori had done an amazing job as there were meats and chesses, salads and fruits and a big cake as well. The table looked great and then Brandon appeared. He looked so handsome and I told him right away as he gave me a big hug as well. Lori was okay with this as she knew I loved him very much and she understood our relationship even though there was no blood between us; we had a mother and son bond. I was thankful for this as it was nice to be ourselves with our feelings after we had now been hanging out for six years. That seems strange as it felt like a lifetime or many lifetimes at that.

My good friend, Sharon, arrived and I had to go and get Lisa but after we all settled in a great manor to watch Brandon. I noticed that there was a great mix of people. From old to young which was one of the highlights about Brandon, everyone loved him. I always had a bit of butterflies during these times and that was just part of it. I didn't see Andrew anywhere or anyone he might have been with so I soon realised he was not here. I did know that he did get a bit jealous with my love for Brandon so it was probably a good thing that he wasn't there. Plus, it was nice to hang out with Sharon. She is really a great friend and I'm thankful to have her close to me.

By the time of Brandon started his third set, all the kids were on the dance floor and it started to get a little crazy. I, all of a sudden, found myself up near Mark (the drummer) and Brandon sort of standing by Mark. I probably would have been closer to Brandon but he was close to the wall and people were all around him. I was wishing I had a shirt that read 'SECURITY! 'It was a beautiful night full of great music, love and wonderful people.

Update

Andrew did come back again and the connection was as strong as it was during the first time we were together. The power of this relationship even with all the things against it was hard to believe even for me. We had a beautiful time together. We played cards, cuddled all night and then spent the day out on the waters of Georgian Bay. I took him out to a beautiful little island on my amazing sea-doo. We sat and drank beer, swam off the rocks and talked a lot. It was wonderful. This was one of the most beautiful days of the summer. We then returned back to my place and I took him home Monday morning. It was the most amazing few days.

Things continued to unfold nicely, and the next weekend, we went back out on the water and then had some of Andrew's friends over to play cards. They were a nice couple and this was really wonderful to experience. The age difference also didn't exist which was nice. Andrew also cooked me dinner as I had some steaks in the fridge. I must say he is an amazing cook and this I am very thankful for.

It was a couple weeks that I started to notice the same pattern starting again. I felt as the closer we got, the more he would pull away. The next weekend, I didn't see him. I missed him but I was busy and just kept going on with my life. Then I heard from him Monday night and he told me he didn't want to make a commitment and there were a lot of women around him but he chose to only be intimate with me. My first thought was yes, me too. Lots of men around and you, Andrew, are the only one I want to kiss. I just replied thanks for being honest because this is the most important thing in a relationship and that's okay, I understood and could see the growth in our relationship He then said to me that he truly didn't know what he wanted and I replied with the same feelings.

As I reflect on this, it was his truth but not mine. I have no idea why I said that. The outcome of this conversation was that I ended up picking Andrew up and we had another great night. Although some more truths came forward that made me question what the heck I was doing. I mentioned this to Andrew and then of course, there was a time for a commitment to come forth as this is really what I wanted and there was a no show from Andrew.

It was a week later that I was out at the bar and my heart was back in control. I have never had to battle my heart and my head so much in a love relationship. And let me tell you, I wasn't doing well with this experience. Yes, not well at all. There wasn't abuse or control, or really anything bad to make me get out of this relationship, it was just my head saying this isn't good for you and you want more verses my heart, body and soul wanting to be close to Andrew. I wondered so many times why God brought me Andrew and I was started to think it was the lesson of battling my heart and soul with my head and my ego. So I asked Andrew to come home with me and he said, "NO."

All my other relationships were great at this moment as my consciousness remained in all of these relationships. Even my relationship with my sister and her family was improving. This really warmed my heart as it was nice to have my family from my beginning back in my life. I do believe my service at my mom's Celebration of Life helped heal some of the wounds with my sister, my niece and nephew which was a great thing as I loved all of them very much.

I was also enjoying the love and healthy relationship with Brandon and his girlfriend Lori. It was so nice just to have an easy relationship with both of them and especially Brandon. We had come such a long way which was beautiful to see. We actually had the strongest love as it was unconditional. There were no rules, no control, no jealousy and no judgment. There was only respect, honestly, joy and love; it was pure love in its greatest form. What an extreme blessing for both of us to experience this type of love in our lifetime.

Maybe we have healed a past life journey of our souls? Maybe all the karmic energy between us has healed? I do believe this is true. You can heal past lives karma in this lifetime. We were now free of any past karmic energy for both of us.

Andrew's birthday was coming up. Knowing he had been there for me on my birthday, I thought it would be nice to be there for him. I got him a card and placed a gift certificate in and went to the bar the day before his birthday. Andrew was friendly and after his shift, he sat down at the bar. I then handed him the card and he was happy to receive it and gave me a hug. Next thing, Brandon and Lori entered the bar and we all had a visit together and a birthday drink with Andrew. I was thrilled and it couldn't have unfolded more perfectly. I left after a bit and I was having dinner at Christine's and my phone went off, and it was Andrew. We talked a bit and I asked him if he wanted some loving as it was his birthday, without a commitment. He was all for that and I picked him up and we had a beautiful night.

The next day, on his birthday, I was planning to go to the bar but God had a different plan for me. I got stuck in a bad accident and it took me five hours to get home from work. I was extremely traumatised as it was a horrific ordeal. The next day, I recovered and then it was Saturday that I choose to return to the bar. Andrew was at the bar Saturday and I was keeping my distance and then he was right beside me. It is so strange how my body reacts when I am close to his. It just sucks right in beside him. We talked a bit back and forth which was nice so I wasn't sure what was going on. He did have a lot of buddies around and a lot of beer in front of him so I decided to leave. I sent him a text saying I was leaving, walking home and that I loved him. He replied that this was another reason why he blocked me: with messages like that. Well, when I read that, it was like a shutter that happened in my soul. How could this man be so compassionate, share such loving moments with me and then say something so hurtful? Was his heart shut down that much? Was he used to hurting people that loved him?

So the pattern continued. I was now texting him, he was reading the texts and not responding. I was trying really hard to let go and I was only doing okay at it. Thursday, I bumped into Brenda in the grocery store and I saw the fear on her face when she saw me. I didn't need to use my psychic ability to see that something was wrong, it was written all over her face. I knew to ask for the truth to come forward and I knew that it would. Brandon was playing at the bar this very evening and I thought how it would put us all back together once again.

I got off work early, headed home and then to the bar. I came around the corner to the front of the bar and there was Brandon. He had quite a few people standing around him as he was always surrounded by a lot of people. It was also the most beautiful thing as I approached the door. Brandon greeted me with the most beautiful hug and kiss. It didn't matter how many people or who they were, the hello was always the same. I then headed into the bar for a beer. Sue was working and we had been reconnecting our friendship which was wonderful. Nothing had happened between her and Andrew and she was just acting from fear or judgment as it comes in many forms.

I then noticed that Andrew popped out of the kitchen, had a look around and all was good. I felt this energy was great. He then finished work and was having a drink at the bar and then he came right over to talk. This was nice and a bit surprising. I even had a little cuddle with him. I thought wow, what a great night this was turning out to be. Brandon decided to play a bit extra and then we had a couple drinks and went to check out another new location for entertainment and then returned to the bar. Andrew was still there and we talked a bit more.

Brandon's buddy did offer to drive me home but I felt to stay with Andrew. I was sort of holding onto Andrew and told Brandon that we had been hanging out again. I explained this because he was like a son to me and I didn't want him to think I was just going home on casual note. Brandon told me he was happy for me and that Andrew was a good guy. Andrew and I then sat down at the bar. He seemed to be on his phone texting someone a lot. He then showed Sue and me pictures of the dinner he had cooked at Brenda's house last night for this girl that had made him a birthday cake. I knew a bit about this girl and I did know she had a boyfriend. Well, something huge happened at that very moment. It was like a sword came down between Andrew and me and cut all the cords. I then had this knowing that I was done. It didn't matter what would be said from this moment on, I was done. It was my heart and soul that was finally done.

We argued a bit as I was walking home and it was said from Andrew that there was no love between us. This did not ring truth but it was what it was and a bye was sent and he blocked me. I didn't have any tears and it was just fine with me. The cords had been cut and I had help from up above. They were not happy with what had transpired between Andrew and me.

The next morning, I felt okay. I didn't feel sad or upset; I just felt like I had my life back or I had my power back. I realised how often in life I had given my power away and that I had done it again. Yes, I had given my power to Andrew and I had finally taken it back. I had also stopped being me. I really can't even believe I did that as it took me years to find myself and I had done great over the last five years, always being me and staying in my power.

As I walked to the bar the next day to get my car, the skies started to rain on me and it actually felt great. I was getting a natural cleansing. I decided to enter the bar and have a drink. There was only one chair left and it happened to be the chair I had just got out of 12 hours ago. The bar was full and I noticed there was the girl that had made Andrew the cake for his birthday, sitting at the bar. She was on her phone texting Andrew from the kitchen as I recognised his logo.

For some reason, it didn't bother me much. Then their food all came out of the kitchen burnt. I knew for a fact that he was responding instead of doing his job. I next got into a conversation with this young guy beside me. He was talking about the entertainment business and told me that besides working for a construction company, he was a stand-up comedian and knew a lot about the entertainment business. I told him I had written a book and a script for this book as this story was going to become a movie. He was quite interested in this. Then Andrew came out of the kitchen for a soda and they said hello to each other and I was completely shocked as this new guy sitting beside me was also named Andrew. Old Andrew looked at me but I didn't react. He then went back to the kitchen and returned a few minutes later, standing beside this girl and her girlfriend. This girl then said to 'old' Andrew, "I will meet you outside." I never moved an inch but confirmation was given why this sword had come down and cut the cords between old Andrew and me. I did see the three of them leave the building but by this time, I was in deep conversation with the new Andrew. He was talking to me about how to protect myself and that I needed to ask for executive producer's rights with my script.

Our conversation lasted three hours and it was one of the most intense and informative conversations I have ever experienced in my entire life. I needed to get a pen and paper to write all this information down. There was a moment that I thought well I shut the door on an unhealthy, not-serving-me-well relationship 12 hours ago in this very same spot and now God was blessing me with this amazing healthy relationship that was good for me and with a new Andrew. I believe the universe was also showing me my books and my movies are my path and my destiny.

I thanked this Andrew and I learned so much about filming, contracts and royalties. When a door closes, another window opens and I would have to say a window closed and a huge door opened as soon as I took back my life and control of who I was.

I thank old Andrew so very much for the time, the loving and the lesson! It was so valuable. I now know that the correct man will enter my life, one that I won't have to stop being me with. I send hugs and a goodbye to sweet old Andrew.

It was a few days later that I really reviewed my amazing encounter with the new Andrew and I knew for a fact it was divine intervention. Divine intervention happens more often then we know and it is defiantly a situation or encounter that is a gift from God.

Love

We know the power of love and that it's the highest vibration and that it keeps us the healthiest. I believe that God gives us examples of this all the time. Brandon had told me a few months ago that he was going to ask Lori to marry him in June at the event party on the dock in Middletown. He said that she made him happy and that he wanted to take the next step in their relationship. I was very happy for him as I felt they both loved each other; they wanted to have a future together and they wanted to have a family. All of this was great and I really liked the idea of a family as I love children and especially babies; yes, the more babies around to love the better. I was also proud of them for valuing their love for each other and showing respect for each other in their relationship. This was and is to this moment beautiful to see.

As the time approached, we all started to get excited for the engagement to unfold. At this time, I still had Andrew in my heart. It just never changes. I also heard that the relationship didn't last with the girl who made the cake. She fell out of Andrew's life.

Time to Pay Attention

After the engagement, Sharon and I headed up to the bar to continue our night. I must say I was also excited to see if Andrew was going to be at there. I had so much love in my heart after watching this magical night. We met up with a couple of kids that Sharon knew on the way. It was nice to talk with them as it's always good to be around the youth and we don't realise how they need that as well. It was like the cottage atmosphere and family type too with all being together. As we turned the corner to the bar, we all noticed there was quite the line-up. It seemed like we all had the same idea. My first reaction was, there is no way I am waiting in that line. I approached the door with Sharon behind me and the first thing I said to the doorman was, "I don't know you."

He looks at me and said, "This is my first night."

I then asked, "Where is Arron?"

He replied, "Who is Arron?"

I said, "The guy with the black glasses."

He said, "Oh the manager."

I said, "Yes, the manager." A few seconds later, he opened the door and let us in. Sharon and I were happy to be inside.

Sharon then kept saying to me, "How did you do that?"

I just smiled and said, "I spend a lot of money in here."

We joined some friends and I was happy to be there. I loved to dance and all was good. I started to look around and I didn't see Andrew, I just thought he wasn't there. This made me a little sad as it really had been quite the night. Sharon and I realised that we had already had a few too many drinks and we did not need any more to drink. I then thought I needed water. As I turned to the small bar area that was right behind us, I then saw Andrew sitting out on the patio. He was sitting talking to one of the new staff members. She was young, around Lori's age, about twenty-four. The first thing that I noticed was that he looked happy. He was just shinning and enjoying talking with her. I didn't know if there was anything going on but he looked good and happy. He also had on the shirt I had got him and it looked perfect on him. I remember when I gave it to him and he told me it was a shirt that he wouldn't buy or even wear for himself and now it looked perfect on him. I then had a sick feeling in my gut. Was he to be with someone younger?

Was this the message I was getting over the last few weeks. He did look good sitting beside her and like a good match. It was like my heart was happy for him and then it sank at the same time. I did have such a connection, such a bond with him but all of a sudden, I had the knowing that I probably was to pass through his life because of the age difference. I was to love him so he could shine.

The girl got up; as it turned out, she was working and entered the building and continued to work her shift. Andrew was then up talking with some friends and then there was an upset with a customer. Security was then on the patio taking someone out and escorting him to the front door. As I was looking out onto the patio, Andrew and I caught eyes. He stopped and smiled at me and I didn't really smile back. Firstly, I was a bit emotional as it had been a very special but emotional night. I then thought well everything happens for a reason and I was to see him sitting so happily with this young woman. I just felt that I had to let him go as I wasn't the correct match for him.

Andrew then came into the bar area and stood close to me but I was not able to look at him. I did look really good and I could tell he was happy to see me but all my walls had gone up and I was listening to my head again. It was like I was busy placing all the blocks the closer he got to me. I next thought, was I jealous?

I had already been to Lisa for a healing after the first time I got really jealous with Andrew. I knew I still had more healing to do from my past marriage as well. Andrew did bring up healings that needed to take place from my past. I thought well maybe I was still even carrying around past pain from a past life. Maybe I had been cheated on in many past lives and that feeling was now in my essence? Whatever it was, I didn't like it and I wanted to get rid of it. I then remembered Rob saying I needed to heal my heart chakra. I agreed with this statement and I had the awareness and I knew he was right and I had tried to heal it and here it was right back in my face again. I also knew that my ex-partner had really done a job on me. I had forgiven him but there was a lot of damage to repair after you have been through something like I had been through.

Andrew then took a seat right close to me as if he wanted to, he could have reached out and touched me. He seemed quite sober which was nice but not me, I was a mess. Then Tommy started playing the song, *Shape of You,* and I really like that song and I started dancing up a storm. I loved to dance and I was very good at it. All of a sudden, I felt this not really love tap but a good strong tap to my butt. I turned a bit to see Andrew passing by and I guess he felt the urge to slap my butt. I didn't even acknowledge it and I keep dancing. Sharon then told me that she needed to go home as she was done for the night. I thought I should go home with her and then I thought I couldn't leave. As soon as I am around Andrew, I can't leave and so she left and I stayed.

I felt a little lonely when Sharon left. I really wanted to have some support from a man in my life. Andrew was here and close but wasn't a sure thing or a steady commitment. He didn't know or care what I had been through that evening and was definitely not by my side, as I could have really used a little support this evening. This also hit hard and I was now going through some big awareness during this night. I can hear a voice inside saying this is why you are in a twin flame relationship to create growth within both of you! Yes. I had just watched love, respect and support within Brandon and Lori's relationship that even though I was older, I still wanted that. I wanted that special love in a relationship and I was settling for nothing at all like that with Andrew. I wasn't even talking to him or seeing him at all. The only thing that was happening to us was when we were in the same room, which only happened when I showed up at the bar, we would have this bond or connection between us. The love did come forward and it was strong but were we a good match? It wasn't that I didn't like to be at the bar, dance or have a few drinks, our interests were the same that way but our wants in a relationship were different. He was young and still playing the field and I was mature with knowing exactly what I wanted and needed in a relationship. This was also an important awareness for me. I knew exactly what I wanted and my relationship with Andrew was extremely far from it. I then thought why did this young man come into my life? I know the moment he saw me, he fell in love with me. He then sat beside me for a year until I finally took him home with me and, once again, the intimacy was so strong that very first night that it is still in my essence. Many a time, I say to myself what the heck and why the heck has this happened to me. I sure didn't want to be with someone I didn't trust and who didn't have respect for me and who didn't want to be with me, and only me, no matter what the age difference. So now I stopped in my tracks and I thought well yes no matter what, the love was only still hurting my heart and not healing or moving forward in a relationship that was healthy for me. I was settling and that was not where I wanted to be at all.

Father's Day

I didn't have plans for Father's Day and I knew the day would unfold perfectly as each day does. I am thankful I have reached this place in life because I used to have the need to plan everything and every moment. I also, at times, believed I should have been somewhere when I was not but with my consciousness, I learned if I was to be anywhere, I would have and that is that. I went to bed peacefully knowing the day will be amazing however it unfolds.

I slept in to 9:20 which was a treat. As I woke up, I checked my phone and I had received a message from my amazing hairdresser, Michele. She has been in my life for twenty years and has been such a wonderful part of it. We always have had a loving and beautiful relationship. It read, 'What would you like with your coffee a bagel or a muffin?' The first thing I thought was how great to have a visitor this fine morning. I then thought to myself that I hadn't made a hair appointment and maybe she was just coming for a visit and wanting to talk about Brandon's engagement. I replied that I would like a yogurt and a green tea. I had been off coffee for the last few months and no bread either and my stomach was doing much better. Michele replied with a laugh out loud and an okay.

I then got out of bed thinking this is nice having company coming. It was a few minutes later that I started wondering why Michele was coming to visit. I was thinking of doing my laundry and going to do a few errands and I was sitting in my faith. I was outside fixing things when Michele pulled up. I greeted her at the car and she handed me the coffee tray and I was glad to see her. She then said, "I will grab my hair cutting things." I thought to myself, I guess I am getting a haircut. I also remembered I had thought a couple times this week that I should call Michele and here she was. So then I thought if I am that good at manifesting, I will ask for my script to sell and for my man to appear. I smiled within and we both entered the house.

We cozied up at the kitchen table, served our breakfast and started to chat. We had such an ease with our conversation, it's so wonderful to be with each other. I was thankful God and the angels had sent her and I was going with the flow, as I believed everything happens for a reason and we were meant to being having this visit. We first started to talk about Brandon, how happy we were for him and how much he had grown over the years. Next, it was all about my girls and Christine as well, as Michele knew how much I loved Christine too.

Then the conversation turned to Michele and what was going on in her life. She started to tell me her partner was quite sick with cancer and that she had a small tumour in her throat area and they were going to remove it. I was sad at this moment and I knew it was time for me to listen to Michele, as listening is one of the greatest gifts you can give someone. I was also holding space for her sending her light and love.

We then moved to the living room and I received a wonderful haircut. Our conversation continued in a loving, healing manner. I then paid Michele and she headed on her way. It was a few days later that she sent me a message saying she had mixed up the names and had arrived at my house by mistake this Father's Day. I just laughed and explained I thought she was there for a reason and thanked her for the wonderful haircut I received.

It has been Raining Men

All of a sudden, it has been raining men. The men seem to be everywhere. Now I must say I have lost fourteen pounds and I am looking pretty hot and they are all around and everywhere. As I sit at the bar enjoying the music and watching the hockey game, a man enters the bar and sits behind me. The people beside me leave and he takes a seat beside me and sits very close to me. I'm a friendly person but I find this a little uncomfortable. Brandon is the live entertainment so he comes over and gives me a hug and a kiss which helps a bit. I feel the need to explain to this man that Brandon is like a son to me. He smiles at me and then keeps getting closer and closer. He tells me he is single and lives at one of the beaches in the area. I keep getting closer to the far side of my chair and Brandon sees the strain on me and comes in with another visit and this helps a bit. I almost think this guy thinks I am going to go home with him. First of all, this is not going to happen, no way at all. Really, during this time, I'm missing Andrew and when my heart is connected to one person; it's connected to one person. He finally gets the picture that I'm not going home with him and pays his bill. He then kisses me on the lips and tells me he will be back for me. Like, really, can you believe that?

Now the next night being Friday, I'm at a fundraiser for the kids in our town. Kids everywhere need help and in our small town of Middletown; they need a lot of help. The people running this event and the programs supported are a home for our teenage youth that still need to finish their high school years and my beloved Face Program. I have been a volunteer for the Face Program for many years and Martin Prost, the founder, saved my life a few years ago. The Face program is a diversion program from the court system for our youth that have committed small crimes such as theft, drugs and assault. They really are not small crimes but they happen often and the police cannot keep up. I believe a lot of these crimes have to do with our society and the agenda of the people in control of the world. This event is called the Battle of the Bands.

Now there are two men that come up and start talking to me and one of them stands very close and starts to dance a bit with me. The other one is watching from the side. It's now that I start to think something is up. I keep my distance and this man backs off a bit. I stay for a few songs, talk to Martin and his lovely wife Beth and then quietly leave the event, I then head to the bar. I notice that my girlfriend, that I am not too sure about, is working the main bar and I don't see Brenda. I'm sad as I am very fond of her and I have always got along well with her. I, all of a sudden, see she is working the floor as a cocktail waitress and I'm so happy to see her. She gives me a big hug. I then ask her why she was out on the floor and she tells me she is having some surgery and would be off for the next two weeks. I get sad about this as I love most of the staff but I am really fond of Brenda as she has a spirit that you just like to be around. I say hello to Roy, he is the owner, and as it's his 50th birthday, I have a card for him. It's a little tense with Roy, as I don't think he was very happy with Andrew and me hooking up because Andrew works for him. I then head to the side bar to get a Corona. Krista is working the back bar and she is also a good friend. I am standing to the side dancing with the music. Tommy is the DJ and he is doing a great job. Right away, there is this sweet man standing beside me and he asks me to dance. I agree. He seems quite drunk but we manage to have some fun on the dance floor. Tommy is nice and plays my favourite song at the moment this being, *Shape of You*, by Ed Sheeran. Brenda passes by and we have a bit of a dance, which is fun.

Brenda continues to work and I return to where my beer is and this nice looking man, about 50, is casually swaying from side to side. He then approaches me and is now hanging off of me asking me to dance. Chris, who is another favourite, passes by and I say, "This guy is really drunk." I probably shouldn't have said that because Chris is one of the guys on security and it then became his job to remove him from the bar. There appear three more security bouncers around him and I really feel bad. He then turns to me and says, "I have been alone for 10 years so I am always looking and trying" and then he walks away. My heart sinks as there are so many people alone. Brenda, at this time, is passing by. I ask her for a piece of paper and I write down my number and give it to her. Just then the drunken guy gets escorted out of the bar. They did call a cab for him, which was the best thing, as he had had too much to drink and I really wasn't in the mood for having a nice drunk man hanging onto me. Brenda passes by again and I say to her, "I don't know what is going on as there are men everywhere."

She says, "Is it raining men?"

Well, I just start laughing out loud and say, "Yes, it is but my heart belongs to Andrew and there is nothing I can do about it."

She says, "I am cheering for you both." This almost makes me cry and is nice to hear. Andrew and I sure had a lot against us. Age, us from different worlds, past pain, alcohol, drugs, him never being able to commit but we had love and an unbreakable connection.

While working in a frequency clinic, I have learned everything there is to know about vibration and frequencies and the human body. I understand that the human body is all about vibration and energy. Its stress, carbs, sugar, chemicals in our foods, water and air and, of course, the bad frequencies that we get from the wireless and cell phones that lowers our body's vibration. It is also the daily newspaper and evening news with the extreme negativity of the world that lowers our body's vibration. It's the hurt we cause each other and the extreme dysfunction within relationships that also affect the body. The body is really made to heal itself but if our vibration is low, our bodies are frozen and unable to heal themselves and function as they should.

What brings up the bodies vibration? Take a plate of salad vs a plate of French fries. Which do you think brings up the vibration of the body? Of course, it is the salad. There are many high vibrational foods that bring up the vibration of the body and help the body work better. Positivity also helps bring up the vibration of the body, so get rid of the negativity because it is making us, the people, sick! Next, the highest vibration is love! Love and the power of love is the key to everything. And right now, I am having an 'Ah ha' moment because I am now experiencing love for myself, working on self-love and that is why it's raining men. My body is vibrating higher than it was before I started in the relationship with Andrew because I have learned more and experienced love from a twin flame. I have so much self-love in my life right now that my body's vibration is higher and I am attracting the men. My light is also shining brightly as we have an aura and mine would be extremely bright because I have connected with my soul as I believe the connection with Andrew is from the soul. Also, because of my level of consciousness and the work I have done on myself has helped with the brightness of my aura.

I wonder how this is working for Andrew. Is it raining women for him too? I feel it probably is. He has never felt love and let me tell you the love has been very strong between us and, therefore, he is now vibrating at a different frequency, a higher vibration and a higher frequency. Before our separation, he told me he had lost weight. I knew it was due to the higher vibration of his body that it would be working much, much better. He also told me that all of a sudden, everyone wants to take him home. I really wasn't too happy with that information but at least we have an honest relationship that we are able to tell each other everything. As I look at him now, I do see that he is shining, his light is shining and his smile is brighter and I know it's because of love. If we, as humans, realised the power of love and how it can affect the body and the consciousness of the world, we would live in a better place. We are all connected and raising our individual consciousness helps everyone. If we could only change the vibration of the world to more love! I know the human race would be healthier as the human body would be working better and there would be less sickness.

All I seen at work for the last four years is one sick person after another. It's so sad. I try to educate every one of them with the knowledge of vibration and frequency. I tell them love, laughter and funny movies are all part of their homework. It's all connected and we are not told that because of the people in control want to keep us sick. It's all about the money and it's sickening. And the only way to fight this is to become the light as Martin Luther King said, "The only way to fight the darkness is to be the light!" He was so right and I'm not even sure if he knew the depth to this statement and how important it was to mankind.

I once again wonder how Andrew is doing with all these women around him. I do believe his light will dim if he doesn't respect the love between us. You don't pick who you fall in love with and when you have that soul connection, it's one of a kind, and it doesn't disappear. Also if that happens and I hope it doesn't, I don't believe those relationships will last because they are not from the soul.

So now we go back to the test of love. Will the love between Andrew and me prevail? There is nothing I can do about it but keep going on my life. Writing, working, being with family and let things unfold and at least I know what I want from the relationship the next time with Andrew. I also know for sure not to jump into another relationship and go looking for a substitute way to fill the void. We do know that people come into our lives for a reason if we are only aware of it and paying attention. I also know that if I went home or took home another man, the sex just wouldn't feel right either and why would I want to put myself through such pain. I am staying with love and having faith with the power of love until I find out there is a decision made in another direction. I just don't know how Andrew is doing with his aura shining brighter and his body vibration at a higher frequency? Or how he is doing with the situation that it's raining women!

The Answers Came

I was having such a hard time understanding what was happening to me and why? I just couldn't understand what was going on? Why I was still so connected in my soul with Andrew. Here I was this a mature woman, I had lived in a million dollar home, had all the toys, raised two successful children, had written and self-published two books, volunteered in my community helping kids in trouble and I was a successful healer, and I was in this relationship that made no sense. I was at the stage that I was thinking about Andrew 24/7 as the soul connection was so intense. I also couldn't understand experiencing such love one night and then one week later, you experience such distance, everything didn't make sense and something was wrong. I like the Adele song where she says, "Let me down easy but don't tell me you don't want me," as this is exactly how I felt. Now I was asking for the answers to come.

I then had a calling to go back to YouTube and review what I had learned about twin flames. It reinforced how painful this was which I already knew and understood quite well. Then I continued to understand that we were both growing during the time of separation which I also knew was true. Then I came across the information on having faith and trusting the outcome. This stuck with me and I knew this was what I had to do. This was another and the most difficult test of faith, I had mastered faith in all other areas of my life and in all other relationships I guess it was now time for faith in a twin flame relationship.

A Strange Phone Call

I received a call from a good friend of mine, Joan. She was in need to talk to someone about the situation with her partner and her marriage. Joan explained to me that a girlfriend of hers was texting her partner and wanting to meet up with him at her home. The time for them to meet was during the day when her partner was at work and her kids at school. I firstly just listened as she was very upset. She then went on to say that she understood this woman wasn't happy in her marriage but didn't have to ruin another marriage. I then opened up to Joan that something similar had happened to me in my past. Now from a place I know of and believe in, it's not really correct or appropriate to text your girlfriend's partner or husband. Let alone talk with him about hooking up. Like, really, have the people gone mad? Have we lost knowing what is right or wrong? And do we need confirmation from others? Has evil turned into okay or good and is it even accepted now?

It is the very next day and for some reason my plan of action to stay away from the bar is just not unfolding the way I thought. When you plan things and say you are not going to do something, you at times get tested on this situation. It's not Brandon's Thursday to play at the bar and of course he is playing. I would have to say I knew or had a strong feeling he would be playing for some reason on this Thursday and it would bring all of us back together in the same building once again. I did sit quietly for a moment and saw how I felt about it, see what my inner spirts and instincts were saying. They were definitely saying that I was to go. I was to get there a bit late and that I was to leave when Brandon was finished playing. This felt right and this was what I was going to do.

It was a funny feeling walking towards the bar. I had had such fond memories towards finding the amazing friendship that I had with Andrew. As I entered the bar, I noticed Brandon was on a break. There was no sight of him, therefore I knew he was in the bathroom. Sue saw me right away and she had a strong level of smugness about her that was noticeable.

Brandon was going for a smoke and I decided to approach the bar for a beer. Sue seemed nice and I asked for a Corona. She got me one and I paid cash and took a seat at a table across from the bar and Brandon returned to his keyboard. The spot I took was perfect as I had a great view of the TV with the hockey game on and a good view of Brandon. The kitchen door opened and I did see Andrew. He looked good and was working away. He did see me and I do feel that it stopped him a bit in his tracks. It was like both of us felt the same way and this could probably be truth as if we are a mirror and if we have both created this relationship; we were mirroring exactly how we both felt at this very moment. It was sad that we were apart but knowing we were from different worlds, we wanted different things and there was an age difference, it probable was better for both of us to be apart.

I could also feel the love in both our hearts that we were trying to let go of and deal with the beliefs that were keeping us apart. I could also see that he was happy in his life as I was in mine. I enjoyed watching Brandon and was enjoying myself too. Then I could feel Andrew looking at me through the window and the pain he was feeling. There was no way I was going to look that way. I had been hurt and there was no way I was giving any energy that way. I do still believe he had been manipulated into having nothing to do with me and he was listening to others, following his head and ignoring his heart. I was glad at this time that I would be leaving in an hour. I was also thankful I had Lucia and Lisa on text and I had support all around, even though I felt like I was surrounded by the darkness. Lucia a co-worker was making me laugh by asking if Sue and Andrew were there. I texted yes, all the characters were present for this scene.

I was enjoying the hockey as it was a good game. Montreal was playing and I am a Toronto Maple Leaf fan but I was still cheering for them. It was also overtime so it was exciting and Brandon was playing at the same time. Therefore, it was turning out better than I thought. Sue was still being sweet as could be which even more showed her true colours. I could still feel Andrew's soul but he was hiding in the kitchen. He probably should have been done work but he wasn't coming out of the kitchen. When Brandon finished and was all loaded up, I went and paid my bill. Sue was still being sweet as anything and then I left the building.

I cried on my way to the car. My heart hurt and there was nothing I could do about it but let the pain out. I had been through so much and all I wanted was to be in a loving romantic relationship so I could just love someone. I had a reading booked with Francis the next morning and I was praying it would give me some answers and some direction.

The next morning, I woke up with Andrew still in my heart, it just never changes, and it never goes away. This twin flame connection was strong, stronger than I thought was possible; at least I was thankful I knew what it was. I had to keep busy and enjoy my life with staying in faith. Faith was the only thing that was going to get me through this.

My reading was great with Francis. It was mainly about my destiny with being an inspirational teacher and a healer. She also explained that God had chosen me to be this amazing healer and that it would be big, very big. This warmed my heart and scared me a bit too although it's an honour to be chosen by God to help the people of the world. I did ask about Andrew and Francis left it kind of vague as recently the readings said I would have him forever. She just said he was learning and growing and I guess that was all I was to know at this time.

This day became a little tough as I knew my greatest and most important relationship was with God and I was okay with that. I just kept talking to Him, trusting I was going through what I was to and I was experiencing what I was to experience. I then decided to visit my good friend, Stephanie, I was thankful our friendship had survived the tests of life. Plus, I really couldn't imagine my life without her. On my drive there I felt this connection with God getting stronger and stronger. I knew if I was going to be this amazing healer, I must let God flow through me. I still wanted a wonderful man by my side and I was trusting God would place all the correct people around me. I then felt as if I was moving up into another level of consciousness and this felt good. I understood and taught the power of love so I decided to send love to everyone, even Sue. I knew that to raise my consciousness and to be in the consciousness of all the other great master healers had obtained, I had to stay in the essence of love within myself.

I had been tested with this concept of sending love to Andrew when we are apart and I had not done well. Not well at all. I had great growth from that experience and I thank him for that. Staying in love is the key to making your dreams come true as this is how you connect your energy to the universe. I keep seeing and saying my script is sold as this is the first thing that is to happen for both Brandon and I, as we are together and separate in our futures. Now it was my test and my goal, it was to stay in the essence of love no matter what happened to me.

As I arrived at Stephanie's I felt at peace due to the majestic view of nature that surrounded her property. I got out of my car and approached the front door. She greeted me on the porch with a hug filled with love and friendship. I held on tight as a few tears ran down my face.

More YouTube

Back to YouTube I went as this twin flame connection was not leaving me. I had confirmation again that Andrew is the runner in our twin flame connection. It was explained that they are not ready to work on the issues needed for their soul's growth so they run. Sometimes they also 'RUN' because they're scared of feeling such a powerful connection to another person. This is Andrew for sure. I know he has never felt such a strong connection as he told me this himself. This is unbelievable and true and I know something we are both to experience! I still can't believe at times that this is happening to me and with someone that is 20 years younger than me. Then they explain that the separation stage can happen several times during this relationship. I look up to God and say, "I sure hope not because this is very, very painful." It does make sense though that Andrew doesn't want to work on things or issues to help his soul wit growth. He has lived and operated from his ego always in this lifetime. It isn't totally his fault as he never was taught or learned how to live and operate from his soul. He also has no idea what to do with the love and the connection he feels for me, especially since I am 20 years older than him. Wow, that's really something to happen to a man. I feel for Andrew as my past belief system almost feels his pain. I guess I need to do some more work on my belief system.

Sometimes twin flames are to also ignite something within each other. Well, this is exactly what happened between Andrew and me as my fire is lit within and his must be too. Yes. for Andrew I feel our relationship ignited life back into him. I believe his childhood sucked most of his drive and joy of life out of him. He now felt alive and at sometimes as if he was twenty again. He even started to regain his looks and body type when he was in his younger years.

Next it says that the twin flames are the physical embodiment of God's love. Love is the whole reason behind the creation of twin flames. Therefore, true twin flames would never come together if their union was to cause pain to another person. This is good to hear because our union did not cause pain to any another person, it only brought joy and love to Andrew and me and really love to others. I do believe that our love is just being tested and it will prevail and even though there is an age difference; it will be a beautiful union and one that will last the rest of our lifetime.

It helps that I believe that if I am going through this. I am supposed to being going through this. I can see myself doing some counselling in concern with relationships and someone asking question about this pain in their heart and this inability to let go of someone and I will be able to say, "Oh yes, I totally understand." I wonder at times why God puts me through so much pain. I have been through a lot and I have experienced tremendous growth almost more than I thought possible. I have learned to live my life from a place of love and I understand the power of love, therefore I want to teach it. Moreover my book, *Just Being There*, is based on the power of love. I see this script sold as a movie and the filming starting soon. I have this knowing of the power of love in all areas such as my children, family members, my girlfriends and all the extra people in my life. I know and understand that I am learning this in the love relationship area and it makes sense that I would be going through and learning about soulmates and twin flames. I just wish the age difference wasn't so big but it makes sense that my situation would be even harder to see if this twin flame is valid and as strong as I have learned. It does make sense with the feeling in my heart and my soul connection with Andrew. Therefore, I am hanging in there and waiting to see the outcome of this love connection and in the meantime, I am working on me. I see that the twin flame is a soul stream of connection of the same level of consciousness. I always knew that Andrew had a high level of consciousness; he just wasn't applying it to himself. That's why we connected in the first place and why we became such good friends.

I have learned more about twin flames and I find it very interesting and it's opening up great awareness. First, there are many problems between twin flames and this causes heartache and pain within. It is like you know you are to be together and you are not and it is a very strange feeling within. You think about your twin flame often and always if that makes sense. I now know that you are to grow your consciousness between the two of you in the love or relationship realm and to heal your ancestors' past pain as well. Your souls are the same as from the same stream or soul group and are to be as one on earth to create oneness on earth. When connected, you both have a strong purpose on earth and this is to help mankind. This is the power and proof of God and is also the battle between good and evil. I once again see the post that is on Andrew's wall of 'once two souls are united' this would be the soulmates, twin flames 'the devil finds ways to keep them apart'. I am learning the depth to this statement more and more as I learn more and more about the truth and the agenda between this. If you read the Bible and understand the darkness and the dark side wanting control over the humans, you will understand that it has always been the fight between good vs evil or God vs Satan on earth. We must have awareness of our twin flame and know how important it is to create a solid relationship with our twin flame to help mankind with raising the consciousness of mankind. This creating oneness for the two souls and raising the consciousness level of the world which creates a healthier and a better world to raise our children in. Once you understand the outside forces, you will understand the importance of the connection of the twin flames and the survival of this relationship. I wish I could share all of this with Andrew and thank him for this awareness and the growth that comes with it. I just want to hug him and thank him. He has raised my level of consciousness to a level that I could have never imagined in the relationship realm and I know the importance of these teachings to reach the masses of the world. This importance is to save the world and make it a better place to live, to help our children grow up in a world full of love and to give us more proof of God's existence. The people have no idea how important love is. Knowing its importance, to value it and really the depth of that statement is over the top important. Once again, we need to be with our twin flame no matter what the situation is or what our head or our ego tells us. They have brainwashed is with the media but people are waking up now and this is a good thing. I pray for the day Andrew returns to me as I now see that our souls are the same. We have twin characterises in all areas of our souls. I understand that he's not ready yet but I do know that he is growing, shifting and learning about himself which is amazing to be happening. He has such a beautiful soul and it's just like mine. How wonderful to have met him and have crossed each other's path. Moreover, when souls reunite, we will have a strength that will be from the light and we will be unstoppable. Yes, when we do reunite for good we will be unstoppable.

I now think of Brandon as he is the same soul as me and we are for sure from the same soul group. That's why no one can understand the connection between us. Just stating a fact here and our connection is to raise the level of consciousness as well. We have done the dance and now our souls are as one, even though we are only soul partners not soulmates. No sexual connection at all and there is not to be one.

When Andrew and I do connected and became as one, as I believe it's our destiny and we are meant to be together, our power will be so very strong. We will have the power of God with us and this is what the darkness doesn't want to happen or doesn't want others to see. They are repressing the power of love to keep us in our slave mentally. We must honour and value and work through all the issues with our twin flames and soulmates to save the world; it's plain and simple. Remember this and stop the ego when it tells you he doesn't like you or that there is an age difference, or that there is no way it's going to work. Moreover, remove the games of the ego. Have the faith and do the work.

Being psychic and seeing into the future is really a wonderful gift and something to be thankful for. Wow, it has taken me years to be able to say that as I would have to say at the beginning I had a hard time believing this at first. I didn't understand it and I didn't think it was such a great thing. Then I wasn't sure what I was seeing and what was happening to me. I now know to trust whatever I see and trust whatever I know to be truth. So let's see what I saw with Andrew. I saw that he was also a great healer which really surprised me at first. I was thinking how that could be. Next I saw him and myself travelling together, me speaking as the lead and Andrew speaking as a great healer to the men. I always told him he was to heal the men. He had been through so much as a child and young adult that he had to make it into a positive aspect. I also saw a line of people and I was healing them through my touch and Andrew was standing beside me giving me strength and doing some of the healing himself. I could see the power and the strength that we had between us. I didn't understand it and I wasn't sure if this was a possibility and I know for sure now that I understand that our souls are the same, meaning a twin flame and that once we go through the growth part and became as one, we will be able to fulfil our destiny which is exactly what I have seen in this vision.

What Do We Want In
A Relationship?

It seems to be that this situation has taken a bit of a toll on me, as I find myself this morning in the emergency department of our local hospital. I have been fighting a cold for the past two weeks and it's only getting worse. I know that I have been under tremendous stress with my mom passing and with the on and now off relationship with Andrew. I am learning first hand that grief is an awful thing to go through. It's the loss of the soul connection and I have talked about this before and even written a chapter about it but now I am going through it myself with someone I was very close to and it's not such a nice place to be.

I also must say that as I was driving to the hospital, I started to feel some anger towards the situation. I find myself angry with Andrew and myself because I'm going through everything alone and at times, I don't like being alone. It's not that I am afraid to be alone, it just would be nice to share my life with someone. I just want to have someone to wake up to and to have someone to kiss whenever I want.

I love that line from 'Sweet Home Alabama' and I would like that in my life. I felt like sending Andrew a message saying thanks a lot for being here when I needed you and have a nice life. Funny how we are willing to give up on love so easily or throw it all away? Especially when anger or frustration is the emotion we are feeling. Well, that's really the reason why Andrew and I are having difficulty at this moment. I got angry at something and got mad at him. Now I'm the only one to take responsibility in this situation because I am responsible for my actions and no one else. I tried to control the situation and I tried to control Andrew.

I then thought about what I wanted in a relationship? I had to remember I didn't want to settle anymore even if I was experiencing a twin flame relationship then it would be tough to move on.

Firstly, I wanted a soul connection because I believe once you have that, you can deal with everything. A soul connection is when you know what the other one is thinking, you feel like you are one when you are together and I want to kiss all the time. Plus, a relationship that is non-judgmental, knowledgeable, loves cats, children and family. When you have time you could write your own list of what you want in a relationship, any and all relationships.

Joel Osteen

Trust God in the trouble! This is the topic Sunday with Joel Osteen and how perfect is that because I really couldn't be in much more trouble in my love relationship. I have been watching Joel Osteen for the last five years and he has always given me the answers I have needed to hear. Yes, it's like he knows exactly what I need to hear. It really is quite scary and wonderful at the same time. I'm back from the hospital, having some breakfast and watching Joel. He really is amazing. He teaches consciousness and I'm very thankful for him. He is talking to me, saying that trouble is transportation and this transportation is going to take you to a higher consciousness. I look around, thinking God must be in the room and how could this be happening? I know this trouble in my twin flame relationship is fuelling this book, so there could be some transportation for this bringing consciousness to me and the people that read this book. There could also be the knowing that this trouble could bring strength to our relationship. I know that sounds strange but I do believe this is a possibility and that is really the message that Joel is telling us. Therefore, I will try, understand and trust why I am going through this trouble and try to have faith that it will bring me closer to my destiny and bring more light to my life.

He also says that ordinary people have ordinary situations and anointed people have anointed situations. Well, this lifetime has been nothing ordinary at all in any way shape of form. I have been through so much and yes it has brought me to a higher level of consciousness and I would say closer to my destiny but the love connection seems to be quite difficult place to have trouble. I just miss Andrew so much and all I want to do is love him. I can just feel love all around, like so close but not exactly here. I knew that an amazing man and an amazing relationship was coming into my life and, of course, when it was happening, it was nothing like I thought it would be, nowhere even close. I kind of thought it might be someone my age and maybe someone in business but no, it was someone totally different.

Now Joel is saying to be your best when you are in trouble. This is something that I know and have said in all my books but with the twin flame connection, all my knowing or consciousness seems to go out the door. It's testing my faith and my consciousness! I really feel like saying, "Are you kidding?" I am such an essence of love and all I want to do is love.

Now Joel is saying all the steps are important. All I want to say is, "Are you kidding again? It's important to go through such hard times? Oh right, what doesn't kill you makes you stronger." Is this what it's like down here on earth? So these experiences with Andrew are part of the journey? We are both learning at this time and growing through this?" Okay, I can understand that but it doesn't make it any easier going through it.

This process has started and all I'm to do is stay in faith and trust in God's divine timing. Okay, I am to have faith in love and that this trouble is going to transfer to a higher level of growth and a true purpose in life. Now the test is to stay in my best and at my best. Hard to do with my heart aching but I can do it; it's just another way of being in faith. And I already know that faith is the key!

A Miracle

I had just turned out my light out and slipped into bed when I heard my cell phone go off. I reached over and noticed it was a message from Andrew. It read, 'Hey.' I looked at the phone and experienced a strong feeling of I knew you were coming back. I also felt that everything I had been feeling of this amazing connection was true. I took a minute and responded with a 'Hey'. We started into small conversation and within a few days, Andrew was back at my house. He explained to me that the sex was so good he couldn't stay away. I agreed with him. It was as if no time had passed and our connection was stronger than ever.

I did learned more things from Andrew during this time. I learned firstly that a lot of people that were close to him and that he valued their opinion didn't support him being in a relationship with me. People told him that I was too old for him and made fun of him for being in a relationship with me. Maybe this is why Sue felt she was doing the correct thing by keeping us apart. They believed it was better for Andrew to be away from me as I was too old for him and teased him because he was with me. This really hurt me and then I felt like I had already known this. It was a moment of confirmation of how cruel people can be and of the belief programs that have been imprinted into our minds. I wonder why they couldn't see love and just be happy for the both of us.

I also learned that Andrew has three kids and that he doesn't want to have anymore which I thought was in our favour. It wasn't like I was 40 and he was 20 without children. He didn't want to have more kids so what did it matter how old I was. It doesn't work when others decide what's best for you or judge how someone should live their lives and with whom. Moreover, I am also positive if it was the other way around and Andrew was older than me the relationship would be totally accepted. The good news was that the judgment didn't work as Andrew was back in my life again.

We are continuing to see a lot of each other but now he wanted to keep things a bit more secretive. I could tell there was a bit of a difference but I was happy to have him back.

2018

I was in the grocery store a week ago and there was a woman in front of me with a stroller facing me. This stroller contained a beautiful baby girl around eight months old. I smiled at her and she smiled back at me. Babies are the best and they can tell someone that is operating from their soul. She and I exchange a few more smiles. I then looked over and notice there is more of a family present. I see a partner, a nice looking man and four other children. They are all beautiful each and every one of them. I am once again drawn back to this beautiful baby that is right in front of me and I say to the mom, "What beautiful blue eyes she has."

The dad answers, "Yes, she has my eyes," and the mom and I kind of snicker at each other.

I then said, "What a beautiful family you have," as they were exceptional.

He said, "Thank you and yes, you don't see this very often anymore as the guys are just going to the bar and having children with different women and no family unit is being created." I was studded by his response and silence came over us all but I knew what he said was the truth. I thought about a few guys that I know and this is exactly what has happened to them. They had three children and they all had different mothers. It was a sad moment for all standing there.

I finally responded, "You are correct." He then looked at me with some surprise and a moment of us both knowing the depth it meant for all the children without families. We all were feeling the pain from the children that don't have families and are in pain with missing a parent in their lives and a family unit. The children then started to brighten up the energy with laughter and joy. They then packed up the rest of their groceries and left the building.

As I walked to my car, I knew something had to be done to help the kids of the world. To help the women and the men heal, so that we can remember and live knowing the importance of the family unit.

Why Are Men So Stubborn?

With only having girls and probably because I didn't say much in my marriage, I didn't really grasp that men don't want to be told anything until I experienced more men in my life. I also learned that if you do tell them something, it's more than likely that they will do the opposite. I started learning this with Brandon; he, for sure and to this very moment, does not like to be told anything. Plus, often if I do say something, he does the opposite. It now takes me a week or two to get the nerve up to tell him something from the heart and probably it takes another week or two for him to get over being mad at me. This all taking place with him being a soft soul young man and he loves me. I feel they want to learn everything for themselves and mostly the hard way. Now I let things go except if there is safety in the way because I don't do well when we are disconnected.

From what I remember and maybe it's because I'm a very old soul, we are to balance each other out. The man is the physically stronger of our species and the woman is the nurturer, the mothers and we have strong intuition. This is the woman's greatest gift to help man and he doesn't like it at all. Being a healer, I have been in contact with so many other healers and I can hear them say things like, my grandmother had so much knowledge and intuition. I continually teach and remind people to follow their intuition and most of them look at me and think yes I should have. Well, really all of them. You can see them remembering their gut told them to do something and then they did the opposite and it didn't work out so great for them. I just don't understand why man doesn't take advantage of the strengths of the woman and really to be honest, why men hurt women so much. Moreover, they have been hurting us for many years. Right now, there is so much rape and slavery towards women and children that it's scary. We are to live in harmony that I know for sure and to draw from each other strengths and help each other be successful.

I can remember a time when my ex-partner, I and my two girls were hanging out for a couple days. It was my youngest daughter's graduation from university. I had arrived to Kingston a day earlier with both my girls and we all were staying at my sister-in-law's house, which was very nice of her to put us all up. The first day Emily, Kate and I did some errands and got ready for the next day. We were all sitting in the kitchen after dinner when my ex-partner arrived. It was really quite nice having some family time again. We sat up and talked as family once again. I was extremely happy with my life out of our past relationship and I had forgiven my ex-partner as I had learned on my path of consciousness that you forgive for you. I think it was a little strange for my sister-in-law and her partner as we had a lot of laughs and it was so easy hanging out. My girls went to bed first as I was heading upstairs to my room, I heard one of my daughters asking if I had had fun. My reply was, "Yes it's always nice to hang out with family."

It was very hot the next day and we were all traveling in my car. Emily was driving as she was familiar with the area. The ceremony was lovely and we all were very proud of Emily. We headed back to the car and then for lunch with some of the family. I'm still close with one of my nieces, Coral and she was joining us with her little one, Mabel. The lunch was wonderful and we celebrated Emily's accomplishments as a chemical engineer. As we were leaving, Coral said, "That was a really nice lunch. I don't think I have been around a divorced couple that I didn't feel awkward with."

I smiled and said, "Time heals, I'm happy and forgiveness is important." I was also happy that my daughter got to enjoy her graduation with it being about her.

After lunch we got in the car and I turned up the air conditioning. My ex-partner opened his window all way as he was in the back with Kate. A couple minutes later, I said, "The air is working now and you could probably put up your window." There was no response. I just looked at Emily and said nothing. It was another couple minutes as the car remained hot that I once again asked him to put up his window and still no response. Emily then tried to put up the window from the driver's control and it made him jump. His reply was shocking for me. He said, "Okay, I hear you and it's great that I don't have to listen to you tell me what to do anymore. I can do what I want now." Then he did up his window. The car went silent and I was a little shocked. My first thought was you controlled me most of the time. You did whatever you wanted. You wanted to buy a big boat, you bought it. Every house you picked and even right down to the colour of our bedroom furniture which was dark pine and I wanted the light pine, it was always your way. Of course, I said nothing and it was only a 10-minute drive back to Linda's and I think we all were looking forward to the two cars we were traveling home in.

As soon as I was alone with Emily, I said to her, "Do you remember me telling your dad what to do all the time?"

She said, "No."

I replied, "Neither do I. I barely had a voice then and I rarely said anything. Not like I would now." Yes, it would be a different thing now. I also loved my mother-in-law very much but I could see her telling my ex what to do all the time and she was a little harsh at times but the bottom line is they don't like to be told anything. Even if you have a valid point, they don't want hear it, which is a sad thing. No teamwork at all. Brandon once told me that he had a problem with being stubborn; what a great awareness and something to correct. That could be another reason why Andrew didn't talk to me for such a long time. I did tell him a better way to be and I don't know what came over me and I still feel it was important to get that information out.

The Power of Love

If people only knew what was going on in the world and what energy is available to them through light and love. We are all born with the consciousness of God or Buddha or Zen. It's as we grow that this knowledge is taking away from us. The universe is created in perfect harmony and life is to be in perfect harmony. It has taken me 50 years to get back to the knowing that love and light is the most powerful energy on earth. I have studied so many masters to help get here, Wayne Dyer, Eckhart Tolle, Louise Hay, Nikola Tesla and many, many more and it's not just one of them with the answer, it's all of them. They are all telling us the same thing; it is the power of light and love. It may be a little different way with each of them but it's the same message and this message is the light and love and our true power is within. We create our realities with our thoughts and emotions. Yes, our thoughts and emotions are to be tools to assist us with manifesting whatever we want to experience. With most humans the mind and their emotions are running the show. If we only used our thoughts and emotions to work for us with our souls in control the world would be a totally different place.

Andrew and I were still enjoying each other with playing cards, going places and just being together. We had an ease that was wonderful to experience. When we were together, there was no feeling of an age difference at all. We were just two people enjoying each other. The way it should be in a relationship.

Staying Focused

You know when you just know something and you just know it. It's like I know and I have for the last 10 years that I am to be a spiritual teacher and a healer. I have known since I was a child that I had the ability to heal and guide others. I started knowing things, seeing inside people and getting messages at a very young age. I let that go when I was 19, as I had no one in my life that had any background of being psychic so it was a lonely path. It was when I was thirty that I started connecting with my knowledge within. When I was 40, it was time to wake up and start to walk the path of the knowledge that I had. There are many people that know they are to do something profound in their lifetime but many don't walk the walk. If it is with being a musician, a poet, a writer or a healer, they just don't pay attention to the knowledge of their destiny.

I must stay with Andrew in my life and the fact of me wanting to always have this special love between us, I am diverting from my path or losing my focus. If you are in a relationship at this moment that is stopping you from your path, mission or destiny, please sit back and take another look. Realise if you are focused and on the correct path. Learning to stay on your path without giving up your purpose and destiny with being in an intense relationship or twin flame relationship is very important. Once again it is finding balance and not losing you in any relationship for both male and female.

The Heart Wants What It Wants

Life would be wonderful at times with Andrew and then it would follow a pattern of him being in and out of our relationship, not wanting to commit or really, at times, acknowledging that he was in a relationship with me. I accepted it and continued to love him unconditionally. At this time, there was a Selena Gomez song that I started to resonate as truth for me. I know in my life I fought my heart for a long time before I moved to the next level with Andrew. Then it was magnetic as the song says, "You got me sipping on something I can't compare to nothing." Well, that's exactly what was going on with me. Then, "I am acting a bit crazy," which is exactly what happened next to me too. I love the line, "I'm praying that I'm going to get out alive." This is truth! Also, "The bed is getting cold and he's not here. There are a million of reasons I should give you up BUT the heart wants what it wants."

"Save your advice because I won't hear it. The heart wants what it wants. Now lighting me up like Venus and then you disappear and make me wait." This is so true and something I don't like at all. One minute he is here with me and the next he is gone. Next, "Finding a way to let go baby, baby no I can't escape; yes, it's so hard to let go of what the heart wants." What a brilliant song! There is just so much truth to this; your heart and your soul know exactly what it wants. Plain and simple, it's always plain and simple. We just seem to make everything complicated and we judge. Judgment is just not good for anything or anyone. I do pray for a happy ending for Andrew and me. It's time for the soul, the heart and for love to prevail. It's time for the love to win instead of the evil in relationships or the old beliefs that have been brainwashing mankind for centuries.

Do we choose to stay in love and value love? They say if we didn't have choice, we wouldn't value love. It does change everything and shit happens; this I know for sure and are we willing to give up on it so easily?

Getting close to the end of the song the lines are… "This is a modern day fairy-tale, no happy ending, no winds in our sails? Is this what they want us to believe? Or is this the way it is? Once again, they keep us small as slaves and out of love. I cannot stress the importance that we value love and we have to stay in love no matter what it looks like. It's really important for our economy, our children, our grandchildren and the future of the world. I just truly wish and pray that we get back to honouring and valuing love.

Most Important Relationships

The most important relationship we have is our relationship with God and ourselves. We come into the world with this relationship in place and due to the brainwashing, the chemicals in the air and our food, we lose the inner connection with God. Then it's a fight with the darkness to keep you in your ego and for some of us to sell their souls. The unseen battle that has been taking place always is for the soul. The light then has to regain this relationship with God and reconnect with your soul. This is the Holy Spirit that lies within. When we are in a healthy relationship with ourselves and God, we connect with the God within, your Holy Spirit and also called your higher self. This means we find the goodness and the love within us that has been calling at us forever to listen to it. This is truly the backbone for everything. As I have stated above, it is all about reconnecting with God within and the power of it. We are given little hits and examples of it all the time and all over the place.

How do you connect with God and the God within? It first of all starts with understanding what God is and what knowledge our souls contain. We are giving this Holy Spirt within and told about it and what is it all about. God is love and we know that there are only two emotions, which are fear and love, therefore if we are living life from love or God, or our souls, we are living from love. Love being a kind, honest, loyal, trustworthy place. It's very simple, our health and wellbeing is connected to our spirituality; if we are connected to our souls and if we are in the state of love, we will maintain good health.

Why don't they teach us any of this? If we knew that believing in God and having spirituality in our lives would keep us healthy, then why have they not taught us this? We should be taught this in our schools and especially in our churches. I have always wondered why they don't teach us consciousness in grade school.

I once conducted a trial course on consciousness with a grade seven class. It was a friend of mines whom I met on a training course with the Face Program. She was, at this time, emotionally a mess due to many circumstances in her life. I was thrilled when she asked me to come in and help guide her class. I had seven prepared teaching sessions ready for my first visit into the classroom and I wasn't quite sure which lesson I was going to use. As I arrived, I started to move the chairs into a circle formation, which immediately would create a sense of unity, comradery and oneness within the kids of the classroom. The circle formation is one of the most powerful formations to bring people together and build community. The aboriginal people that lived peacefully on this land before us understood the power of the circle and used it often. The kids seated in rows just make it colder and more negative when the kids are learning almost like they are isolated and restricted. I have a saying these days and it's that the world is upside down and this is another area I believe is totally upside down.

We were all seated in a circle formation with the class, me, the teacher and an EA present. Firstly, I started with myself and I gave an introduction about me. Where I lived, about my family, my kids and what I loved to do. Then it was the kids turn to talk about themselves and share what they loved to do. Some loved to talk and others struggled with talking in front of their peers. I let them talk and I could feel tension from the teacher, as I don't think she ever really let them talk or listened to them. Are teachers taught to listen to our kids? The teacher did remove herself from the circle to sit at her desk doing marking and other job-related things.

It was a communication lesson I chose to teach these kids. I paired them up and one had to tell a story and the other had to remember it and tell it to the class. You could see them struggling to listen. I explained that you have to be aware of the ego wanting to make it about them and stopping them from really hearing the other person. Moreover, I taught them to listen without wanting to respond and truly learn to listen. We did the exercise over again and had great success.

Within three weeks, the kids started to open up about their most personal inner life. The power of the circle was unfolding right in front of us. The only problem was that it scared the EA and she ran to the principal. I returned for only one more week. I have bumped into a few of these kids over the past few years and they had a shine about them that was noticeable.

What Happened Next

My heart still wants what it wants and the connection with Andrew has not changed at all.

I go to the bar occasionally and I see Sue and I'm not sure if she knows that Andrew and I are once again spending time together. I know there is fear of losing Andrew as a friend/companion and we can't hold onto other people for our own benefit, as that will for sure backfire. Plus, it saddens me so not having her support when I am feeling so much love for Andrew. I am thankful, at this time, that I do have the support of my kids and the people around me. If it makes you feel good, then what's the problem? Moreover, some say that he's young and he keeps you young which is correct.

Healing Again

I sit and mediate on what has happened. I know the power of the twin flame and what our purpose is but Andrew does not and he's not willing to listen to me. I do believe the age difference was just a bit too much for him. He is stuck in the belief that he should be with someone his own age or someone younger. Maybe it would have been better if it had been 10 years difference and it wasn't it was 20 years. Even though I believe that at the age of Andrew being 50 and me being 70, there wouldn't be any difference at all. Women just seem to age better. I'm alive in my body again and I am thankful for that. I have lost 16 lbs and looking great. The men are everywhere and I am shining just as Andrew is but is it time to let go of this relationship? The feeling of wanting more for myself, what I truly deserve in a relationship, self-love and not settling is back into my awareness.

I also know that many people pass my path and come and go in and out of my life. That is the passage of a healer. It's a bit of a lonely one but because I am a healer, I have an extra strong relationship with God, therefore I'm never alone. I must have chosen this path for this lifetime, knowing it would be tough and I'm just letting God know that in the next lifetime, I want to be married to the same man for 65 years. Yes, a nice and easy lifetime is in order and my karma will be perfect for that.

I feel during this meditation that I am to let go now and try to let go peacefully. There is really no room for anger, as when you live in faith and trust that the correct man will be placed in my path and all will be good. I will be a little bit more careful with the age thing and that's okay.

I think in your lifetime, you only find a few people that really love you and you can trust. We really need to honour love and respect it as I do know that love is the most powerful essence in the world and it is the most powerful healer in the world, and the world is in such bad shape and people are so sick. It's incredible the amount of sickness that is all around us. If we just stayed in love, respected it and valued it, we would be just fine.

Today is a brand new day and a new beginning for me. I am free again as I couldn't ignore my inner awareness of wanting to in a healthier relationship. I'm not jumping into any other relationship or opening up my bed anytime soon. It was an intense twin flame relationship and I need to heal my soul once again. We have to do this on a continuous basis throughout our lifetime. This is also the lessons we learn and the growing of our consciousness.

I also know to let go of any anger, as it may come up as I know my reactions are first to feel the emotion of being hurt and next to anger and there is not more room for the emotion of anger anymore. I have learned this and I am getting much better at releasing anger before it starts. If you live in faith and love, then there is no anger! I just believe it wasn't meant to be and something better is right around the corner.

I just saw a note on Facebook that is so perfect that I have goose bumps it says, 'Honour life's endings, and prepare for something new'. Every ending means a new beginning. This is the truth and something I'm going to do today. Just honour the ending of my relationship with Andrew and be thankful it took place. I'm also going to honour the relationship I had with Sue and not having anything else to do with her and honouring myself as I should. I also deserve a guy that is there for me and Andrew is not so it's time to move forward to a new beginning!

Pain Then Relief

The hurt is still there as I really did feel that Andrew would come back to me and be back to stay. I was praying the love would prevail and the twin flame connection would help mankind. I'm glad that I waited and gave love another chance. That I followed my heart and I didn't do anything stupid and I let life unfold.

I'm going to sit with the pain, feel it and let it pass. I was a little prepared for either way, therefore I'm experiencing a sense of relief today. It's like a sense of freedom that is now filling my soul with hope and a knowing of it's going to be just fine, everything is going to be fine. At least, I don't have to be in an unhealthy relationship that was not serving me anymore and this is great and probably why I am really feeling this sense of relief. I feel relief and at peace. I'm free to be back in my consciousness again and able to live my life the way it should be lived. Due to the inner work I have done, I am able to accept what has naturally occurred. It just didn't unfold the way I thought it would and that's all right too.

Lost Souls

I really do feel that there are many, many lost souls on earth at this moment in time. I also believe that these souls are crying out for help. People are tired of being sick and are tired of the dysfunction and they just plainly want more in life than being a slave to the government that is in hand. I do believe that when we come into this world as babies, we are spiritual beings going to have a human experience. Humans that don't realise this, remember this or learn this, true happiness goes right by them. Are you a lost soul? Do you feel that you live from your ego and that your soul is calling out to you? If so please try and do some meditation. It doesn't have to be anywhere special, just somewhere you feel comfortable. Close your eyes and focus on your breathing. Let the thoughts flow, replace them to positive ones if needed and listen to your soul. Listen and pay attention and do these steps as often as you can.

Soulmates and Twin Flames

Due to the fact I am having a hard time getting Andrew out of my heart and my soul, I decided to do some more research on YouTube. I started learning more about the separation stage between twin flames. I was reminded how painful it was. This was something I didn't need to be told. I had already experienced the pain and now I was experiencing it again and to be honest, not liking it one bit. I look back to what I learned during this uncomfortable time in the past. Joel said, "Be your best when in trouble times." I did that before, it did work and he did come back but he is gone again as it didn't work out.

I then learned this was a time for more growth. Okay, I knew Andrew needed so much growth and I was happy he would be experiencing it. I knew that I was being tested again and I started to accept it. Accepting what is and living without resistance is very important. Yes, living without resistance is key or going with the flow of the river. I had been tested many times over the three years it took to heal from leaving my 20-year marriage to be able to sit without any anger with my ex-partner and actually really feel from my soul forgiveness.

Therefore, once again, I turn to my faith and my strength to be the best that I can be!

Treated Badly

Why do people treat other people so badly? I thought or understood that you are to be kind to everyone, especially the people that you love. Plus, men have gotten away with treating woman so poorly for many years. I just don't get that at all. Women are the ones that bring life to all. We, the women of the world, are the nurtures, we have the intuition and we are the ones you men need to make love to. Why is man so corrupt and why have they repeated the same pattern over and over again? This is why God picked Noah to build an ark and planned to wipe out all of mankind because every last one of them was corrupt. This is the truth of our history. I wonder, are we close to this stage again in history? Plus, if it wasn't for the women, there would be no circle of life.

What do you do when you are in a relationship where your partner treats you poorly? Most of all, what happens when you have children and what happens if those children are young in age? This is definitely a situation where there are no set rules to follow and it's a very delicate situation and each situation is different.

I know of a beautiful young woman that is a good person, a kind soul and a fantastic mother and she is treated poorly by her partner and the father of her children. Most of all, I believe there is infidelity as well. Men are always chasing for something and looking for something that is right in front of them, I just don't get it at all. If they worked together and supported each other, they would have it all. It is like common sense and the teachings of working together works. Why would a man want to have interest with some other woman when he has a wife and a couple kids? If you think it out, if your relationship failed, you would have a wife and kids to support and in these days that would be very difficult. Is it for the sex or the intimacy? Have we lost that totally in relationships? Have we got ourselves into relationships that don't have love in them and then they don't work? And we, as humans, have to work on our relationships and most of all, it is so important to keep the family unit together. The norm nowadays is split families and it's hurting our children. Children need to grow up in a family unit with a mother and father present. We take this for granted so easily. It saddens me and I just can't imagine what God feels like when he looks down on us. No wonder he caused such a great flood and took out mankind. He also gives us so many hints on the secret of life like for instance the word mankind. Like, hey man, be kind, which is the secret of life.

It is amazing that we don't remember anything when we are born on earth. That is our greatest fear when we come into another lifetime that we won't remember where we came from, the knowledge we have within and our destiny we are to have on earth. I am extremely thankful that I do remember where I have come from, even though it happened later in my life. I have the knowledge of God within and over the last 10 years, I have connected with it. I also see my destiny as clear as clear can be. I see myself standing on stage, teaching this knowledge and healing and waking the people up to the knowledge within them. I just have the knowing that men need to remember and connect with the knowledge within and therefore then they would treat their partners well, with respect and integrity as they would want to be treated too. Men carry the fear and we need to eliminate this. If we could only remember the goodness that lies within us, within our soul, we would never treat another human poorly at all or ever. We have already talked about mirroring and we already know that we do mirror each other in relationships. Within many of my relationships I have mirrored jealousy, low self-worth, attachment and neediness.

So what do you do when you partner or spouse is treating you badly? What if you can't pick up and leave the house with the children undertow? What if you are in an abusive relationship? I say a prayer for all of you at this very moment if you are in this situation and you must find a way to get out. You are not to and cannot take physical abuse, it's just something we are not to take or say it's all right because it's not. Therefore, call your local woman's shelter and get a plan in place. When you decide that you want out, the correct people will come into your life and the path will be shown, this I know for sure. As we know, only you can save yourself and we are put in this situation so many times on earth as a test of finding the inner strength that lies within us. God wants us to connect with this inner strength, to raise the consciousness of ourselves and to raise the consciousness of the world as we are one. Therefore, all these experiences we are going through are to raise our level of consciousness and help the earth and mankind. It is just the people in control that want us to stay in the bubbles we are in, so that we continue with our slave mentality and keep making them rich and keep in the dysfunction of the world going.

Now, if you are in the situation where it is not too bad as there is no abuse, it's time to work on you. You are to eat healthy, to walk, to work on your careers, to connect with your soul within and to be the light of God. You are to find that inner strength within to work on you; this is so important to keep working on your consciousness, as when we raise our level of consciousness, it affects everyone around us and it helps the world which in hand helps our children. Yes, if you really want to help your kids and the children of the world, then do the work yourself and became the higher consciousness that we so need. To be the light, by being a good mother, by looking after yourself with the food you eat, read inspirational books, walk more, go on retreats and be aware of the lifestyle you lead; this is also when the correct man will enter your life with a similar soul stream as you.

As I work and work on my consciousness, my life and my connection with the light within I know I will be connected with the correct partner. Therefore, if your partner is not treating you well, then both of your consciousness levels are low and take the first step and work on your consciousness. If he follows you and starts to treat you better, then your relationship has a chance of surviving; if not, he will fall away and you will attract someone with a higher level of consciousness that could be a soulmate or a twin flame. Therefore continue to work on yourself, your spirituality and connecting with your soul.

Moreover, relationships are also about energy, vibration and frequency. Well, everything is really about energy, vibration and frequency. So, if he is not treating you well, then your energy, vibration and frequency is also low and his is low too. This is when negative events continue to happen and poor health happens too. Moreover, if he is cheating on you, then it would be with someone that is at his level of vibration and therefore, it is at both of their losses.

Intermittent Relationships

As I'm writing this book, I am also doing research on all relationships. I have been following Teal Swan for the past few years and a video of hers just popped up on my YouTube feed called, 'Why you are having such a hard time leaving a relationship.' I also feel that it's important to pay attention to things that appear right in front of you when you are asking for direction. So I clicked onto the link. She started off describing an experiment with rats. She was explaining that when they were given love, they also received a pellet with consistency and that all was good with the rats. Then they started to give the connection of love but without the pellet. She explained that they thought the rat would just forget about the pellet but the opposite happened. The rat became addicted to the thought of getting the pellet and the consistency of it. Then she referred it to when someone in your life that you are having an intimate relationship is there one moment and you are talking to him and then he is gone. That that type of relationship is abusive and addictive. Well, I don't know how many lights went off for me but it was kind of like a fireworks show.

Andrew had once stayed over a Tuesday and Thursday night and then when I saw him on Saturday night and he acted as if he didn't know me. I kind of reacted to this encounter a little crazy. There was no consistency and this was exactly what was happening to me. I see it so clearly now. She also said it was abusive behaviour. I know for a fact that Andrew would never do anything intentionally to hurt anyone or me but with his lack of consistency towards me, he was doing exactly that. Plus, I couldn't understand what was happening to me as I had done so much healing on myself and on others as well. How could I just lose all the consciousness I had worked so hard for?

This is exactly what Selena Gomez is talking about in the song I listed above about the heart wants what it wants. Selena sure had a twin flame/soulmate connection with Justin Bieber but when there was no consistency as she says, "You light me up like Venus and then you disappear and this makes me crazy." It's similar to what happened to the rats and really the same thing that happened to me. As soon as there was no consistency, I started to fall apart and lose all my consciousness. Then he came back a few more times and then I became addicted. Like OMG, I did this, this is exactly what happened. Then when it was over, I still didn't want to let go as I still was hoping and wanting that connection because I was addicted to it. What an awareness to uncover and how very thankful I am to have that learning and lesson. I wish I could thank him and I hope millions of people and young women read this book, as it's important that we know that the most important part of any relationship is consistency. If you haven't got that, you have worse than nothing and you are in an abusive and additive relationship. Teal tells you to get out. Get out as fast as you can and start to heal and break the addiction.

Now if Andrew does come back, which he very well could because there still is the soul connection, twin flame and we did experience such love and intimacy, the first thing I would say to him, "I need consistency in a relationship before I sleep with you again. There would be no point starting anything until I can trust you, as when you are not there I will get upset and then the entire cycle will start all over again." I actually feel the same thing did already happen like two or three times. I also hear and feel Selena's pain. It's an easy thing to get addicted to love and extremely painful when they disappear. Not ever doing that again.

I find it ironic that I waited so very long to start a new relationship and then to have been put through all this. Although I am once again thankful for the growth I am experiencing. I knew Andrew came into my life for a reason, he had too because that is exactly the way it works. I also know he needs a lot of healing himself, more healing that I could have imagined any human being could need.

I do wonder how you can have such intimacy with someone and the next time you see them, you act like you don't know them. I do know that Andrew has a lot of problems and has had a rough life but I had no idea about the depth of it. I didn't realise that someone could have the ability to shut off their emotions like that or treat another person that you are to love with such unplanned abuse.

At least I know and understand I must stop settling and not accept a relationship that has no consistency because I will only get hurt and it will make me lose my balance. Then I will get addiction to the love and will lose my consciousness too. And for the men and women that are being there one minute and gone the next in a relationship, sit quietly and ask yourself why you are doing that to someone you love? Is it that you are not committed to the relationship at hand? Or, most of all are you afraid to be consistent because your walls are so high and are you afraid to love, and are you afraid to get hurt or maybe all of the above?

Reflection

What comes to me first is that you fall in love with the person. I think back to my first love and that is exactly what happened to me. I fell in love with the person as we were just sixteen. Jeff was a great guy, kind, loving, caring and trustworthy; he was a beautiful soul and wonderful young man. I also know that it must have not been my path and I'm okay to be exactly where I am right at this moment writing this book. I would have never connected with my soul, my higher self and had the growth that I have experienced. I also fell in love with two other men in my life. They were outgoing, loved to do things and had the love of family. They were a bit different as I wouldn't say they were the same by any means. Randy loved to dance and still, to this day, I miss that. I do believe each of them was a little different and that was the reason they crossed my path. I did leave all three of them which I now know may have had something to do with the abandonment from my father.

I also left Jeff because I was young and needed to experience life. I left Randy because he didn't value me and my ex-partner because I had to save myself. They were all different lessons and they were all great teachers, which helped me raise my consciousness and taught me self-love; we know how important self-love is and that it is the highest frequency or vibration we can be in. I'm also sure they were meant to cross my path and were past lives connections as well.

I knew when I left my 20-year relationship, I needed to heal before I was ready to love again. As I said above, I did try the dating scene three years after, as I was over the separation from my ex-partner and was ready to date. I had two encounters with two men but they were not the soul connection or love that I was looking for or that I knew would someday happen to me. I remember this woman I encountered a few years ago saying that it was 10 years until she found love again and I was like, "Well, if it takes that long, then it takes that love but I would prefer if it came sooner." So I waited and waited and it was okay. I was waiting for that spark to happen again. To feel love again as I knew what it felt like. It had happened to me three times in my life and it would happen again; I just had to be patient. I wanted someone that was kind, loving and conscious, and who wouldn't have any judgment on me and what I had to do in my life. He had to be supportive and accepting of my healing ability. This was really all I was asking for.

It was interesting that Andrew sat beside me for an entire year before our relationship moved to the next level. During this time, I talked to him about my awareness of what was really going on in the world and who was really in control and that we, the people, are slaves. He knew all about it and was such a support. I would look at him and think, wow, I would have never guessed he would be so knowledgeable and he would be so supportive and be here in Middletown. Small towns are usually filled with unconsciousness and people with lack of knowledge. That could be a good reason why I am here, in a place that needs it the most. I would also look into his eyes and feel such comfort and ease. Then I started thinking why is he always there and always sitting beside me?

I knew very well that everyone had a message for you and everyone came into your life for a reason so why was this younger man sitting beside me and why were we getting so close? Sometimes I would think he wasn't even in the building and I would be talking to someone to my left and then I would turn to my right and there would be Andrew sitting beside me. I would at times jump out of my skin and he would just smile at me. After this happened about 10 times in a row, I started to feel this connection with him and I was wondering what the heck was happening to me. I knew the age difference was big but there was a spark and a light within me. I now had the spark I was waiting for and it was with someone I would have never imagined in any way shape or form. I can remember wanting to get rid of the spark as I was listening to my head instead of my heart. That just didn't happen as we know the outcome.

I remember how Andrew was so loving, caring, fun, and funny and he loved my cats. I just started falling more and more in love with him. I fell in love with the person, Andrew. It didn't matter what he had or what he was, I fell in love with his heart and soul. I do believe it was the same for him as he fell in love with me, me the person. I also fell in love with the man that had no judgment towards me. One that supported me always and that was the most important thing to me. Plus, it didn't matter to him what I had because he was falling in love with me for the person I was and I believe this was happening over the year we were together just talking at the bar.

Great News

I heard some great news today! I heard that Andrew is doing well in his life and he is single! That he is not drinking much, not hanging out in the bar much anymore and is looking healthy for the first time in his life. This warms my heart so much and makes me feel that I did touch his life in some way and in a positive way at that. I did tell him that it was him and only him that would save himself. That is the first chapter that I ever wrote in my very first book, *AWPTF Only you can save YOU.* This book is on the games of the ego.

Communication

We know that communication is the key with all relationships as we are to be connected and we are to talk about what is happening within and learn from one another. One thing I say often is, up and out. Yes, up and out with what is troubling you.

Let's talk about communication. We are given this great tool of staying connected with our cell phones but we are less connected with each other on a personal level. Do we sit down and actually talk to each other? Do we express our feelings from a place of love?

I text too much, I know this for sure but I do express how I truly feel in a text message. The scary thing is I believe it has become a habit: to only express how I truly feel through a text message. This is a good awareness for me at this very moment.

I can remember Andrew asking me how I felt about something as we were driving home from the casino. It took a lot for me to speak my truth. Andrew had to encourage me to speak from the heart. It was as if I was frozen and was unable to speak how I truly felt or what I truly wanted.

I believe it was a deserving issue, I didn't believe I deserved to express how I truly felt to his face. This could be an underlining programme I have been running for many years. A belief that I have carried throughout this lifetime and one that I could have even brought with me into this life. What a beautiful awareness that resonates as truth for me.

Have women been holding onto this belief for many centuries? I know for sure that I am going to break this pattern in all areas of my life because if I am holding onto it in the relationship realm, I am holding onto it in all areas of my life. I need to do some work on a deserving issue and the next time I am face to face with Andrew, I am going to speak my truth from a place of deserving and a place of love.

Not Alone

Interesting enough one of my close friends is going through the exact same thing as I am. A man asked for her number and she passed it over to a friend to give to him and they started texting. It was two weeks later that they started dating. The relationship started to blossom and both were enjoying the connection. They experienced dinner out, and from what I was told, things were going well and the connection felt right.

It was in March that my girlfriend and I were heading out to watch Brandon and she told me that all of a sudden this nice man that she had experienced a nice beginning with had just fallen off the face of the earth. They were in a conversation one minute and then he was gone the next.

I have done a bit of research on this behaviour as Andrew has run once before and now he is gone again. So Andrew became the runner and I became the chaser and this was so unconscious for me and totally out of character for me. The only good thing was when Andrew didn't want to hear or listen to me anymore; he would block me. It could have been that he didn't want to hear about a spiritual path or the truth. He did start to fight the path of spirituality and I stopped teaching it to him.

It was the same situation for my girlfriend. Her guy was there and then he was gone. No explanation and she wanted answers. She wanted to know what had happened and what was going on. It didn't matter to her either way, she just wanted to know. I believe he was runner too, and for a short time, she became the chaser. I do give my girlfriend a large amount of credit, as in time, she deleted her guy's numbers so there was no possible way she could be the chaser. She was angry and she didn't want to feel this way anymore therefore deleting and letting go this way was the best route for her.

Two months had passed since my girlfriend had deleted her guy from her phone and we were out having a nice lunch, She told me she wasn't sure if she did the correct thing with deleting this guy from her phone as she missed him. All I could do was smile at her as I totally understood the pain of missing someone you love. She then expressed that she was hoping she might meet him in town somewhere and every time a silver

Honda passed by, she looked to see if it was him. I totally felt for her and understood her pain as mine was the same. She then said, "It's over, it was just a fling."

I said, "No, don't say that, just leave it open. Don't put forth an outcome, as you just never know how things are going to unfold." I could have done the exact thing with my situation but I was going to leave it open and if it was meant to be, it would be.

I also knew that there had to be more to this running and chasing thing and so, of course, I did more research. At this time I was reminded why some run and some chase, this I was all too familiar with. Next what stood out for me was the growth that had to transpire during this stage of separation. The runner is going through growth within him and the chaser has to experience more as well. This growth that has to take place is necessary for the twin flame partners.

At this time I still felt connected to Andrew; even though I knew it wasn't good for me, I was still connected to him. The song of the moment is *I will wait for you;* at this time I was waiting and still working on me.

I, for sure, had my share of not knowing what to do in a love relationship, as I believe Andrew and I met for this exact reason. I know, at this moment, that we are both learning about love and relationships. One lesson could be the same for both of us, this is that age doesn't matter and the judgment of others over age is not going make a difference. If there is love, there is love. We are also from different worlds and this could be a growth area for both of us too. I didn't care that Andrew had nothing, that he didn't have a driver's licence, no bank account, no belongings, three children from different mothers and drank too much, I still loved him. I did take a lot of judgement from many people that he wasn't good enough for me, that I needed someone to look after me, someone that was better than Andrew. Andrew also said to me often the he didn't want me to be his sugar mama, that he didn't care about money and that he wasn't with me because of opportunity. We were teaching each other what we felt was important and this was a mirror of growth for both our souls. He also told me often that he didn't want to hurt me. This was maybe a first for him. We also had to heal great pain from our past relationships from a past life. This is the bliss and magic of a twin flame; as one is growing spiritually, the other does the same. Therefore, as I am working on me, Andrew is working on him. I must have acceptance that both of us need this time and understand that no one can fulfil the self-love that needs to heal within.

Andrew did have to work on himself, his personal growth and take control of his life. I was ahead of him in this area as I worked hard on this a few years ago. This enlightenment I had experienced did set the pace for the runner and the chaser situation that happens often between Andrew and me and the chaser is usually more spiritually advanced. I now live and make decisions from my soul instead of my ego. Plus, Andrew is the other half of my soul as a twin flame, therefore my soul wants to be close to him and at home again. This statement may seem strange but it's the truth. During this time and everything we are going through, could we be creating a healthy relationship? It would be so amazing to have trust in a relationship, no judgment, acceptance of age and where you came from and the intimacy of real love between two souls. Wow, that would really be amazing, wouldn't it!

Unfortunately, my girlfriend's situation ended at this point. I believe she was correct when she said it was just a fling or at least that is what she believed and what she put forth to the universe. We do know that the universe gives us whatever we say. Although I had a few of those type relationships that didn't work out too. They were ones that just were not meant to be. One very important thing I know for sure is when you are in a twin flame relationship, you know it, there is no doubt at all!

Love Thy Enemy!

I seem to be seeing this statement everywhere so I felt it was important for me to pay attention to it and to write about it. I do know, at this moment, that the correct words and message will come forth as I write this chapter but I'm not quite sure of what I am going to write. I will also say that right this moment the sound and thought of the idea of loving the enemy doesn't resonate well with me at all. We are programmed and taught in our lifetime through many wars and terrorist attacks to fight the enemy so no wonder I'm having a hard time even thinking there could be some truth in these three words or that this is a possibility.

Next I look at the three words and sit in silence facing my laptop. Love, I have done a lot of research on the word love over the past eight years. I know that God is love, love is the highest vibrational frequency we have on earth and love is the most powerful essence on this planet. If everyone was in the emotion of love, there wouldn't be any wars or negativity and abundance would be everywhere. It does also come to me that we must have contrast in the world to appreciate or know love. A day consists of light and dark, therefore there must be light and dark in the world. It is what we chose to be or experience in that is our freewill; that has been given to us. Yes, 'freewill' has a lot to do with it. It definitely has been given to us for a reason.

'Thy' is easy, this is thyself. I believe we are to do onto others as we would do to ourselves. Yes, we have heard this before.

Enemy, what really does the word enemy mean? It says someone who hates another. Well, we know that hate is a manmade emotion and it's from the ego. It also says something that harms or threatens someone, or a group of people whom another group is fighting. I do believe we are all one and the same, therefore there really isn't an enemy, and it is only something our thoughts create through our circumstances. I do think it's different when we learn to set boundaries with people and then learn to send them love and light. Therefore, there aren't really any enemies, we just create this term in our minds and no wonder if you look at the movies and TV shows, there is always a bad guy and an enemy. We are programmed to believe there is an enemy.

When I relate the word enemy to my life, I try and see who my enemies are. I know that we are all on our own journeys, learning our own life lessons. Therefore, how could anyone possibly be my enemy? Then I think of the people that are jealous, and I know to have a healthy relationship with them, I keep my distance and send them love, realising I must already know this concept of loving thy enemy. Maybe I need to put it into more practice with the people I do have in my life that I am close to and cannot keep at a distance. These are the people that do not live their lives from a place of love and are stuck in their egos.

Although I still have to protect myself at all times as we are in a world where we do have to protect ourselves always and this has become more apparent in the last 10 years.

I think I am going to continue to practice this concept of loving everyone as when we live from the soul, there are no enemies. We are souls on our own journeys. I will continue to be positive and send love at all times.

Intimacy vs Sex

There is definitely a difference between intimacy and sex. When I was young, I was unable to have casual sex. I just couldn't kiss anyone that I didn't have an attraction to or a connection with. I never seemed to be without sex, as I had my first boyfriend when I was sixteen and we had a lot of intimacy within our relationship. I can remember how electrifying it was the first time we made love. We, for sure, had an intimate relationship that was full of love. I just believe the bond was broken when we were nineteen years of age and it was time to move forward and experience more of life. I did have a few relationships that were full of sex and were not intimate afterwards. Our souls were not connected.

Next I moved out west as this was where my sister and her family lived. I, at this time, believed family only came from blood but now I know family comes from both blood and the heart and soul. This is why I believe so strongly in soul groups and soul connections as well as blood connections. I did read in a book that soulmates and soul partners mostly do NOT come from the same bloodline or family tree. Therefore, I believe you have two strong connections in your lifetime, the connection from your family and the connection from your soul group. This is where intimacy occurs for mankind.

I decided to look up the word intimacy in the Webster's dictionary and I came to a strange conclusion. The definition read, 'the state of being intimate: or something of a personal and a private nature'. Well, this was disappointing. I then looked up intimate, it said, 'to make known especially publicly or formally or to communicate delicately and indirectly'. I like the 'communicate delicately' part; it sort of describes the feeling but only a bit. Intimacy is such love from the soul, it's a one of a kind feeling and it's rare. Maybe this is why the dictionary doesn't have such a true description of it. My conclusion is that intimacy is rare and there is not a valid description in the dictionary because you have to experience it to really know how it feels.

As I travelled out west, I met my next love. There was a strong connection and we started into a relationship. It was a relationship from the heart but there was a bit of a difference than with my first love; don't get me wrong, it was a strong connection but there was just something missing or something that wasn't all there. The sex was great, there was no doubt about that but from what I know now, it was really a strong connection with exactly that, good sex. We had a different belief system and I know that after a few years, we ended up going our separate ways just because it wasn't a true connection from the heart.

I then found myself back in Ontario and living with my mother once again. My sister had also moved back and this was where I was to be, close to my family. My girlfriend that I had travelled with and had ended up out west with had moved back to Ontario and she was working at a restaurant in Mississauga. After I rested a few days from my drive across Canada, I decided to go and visit her.

It was a beautiful brand new restaurant that was very large in size and seemed to be very busy. Jean was glad to see me and I was glad to see her too. I sat at the bar and she introduced me to everyone she knew. It wasn't long until I met the owner of this restaurant. He was just a bit older than me and it wasn't long until he offered me a job as they were looking for experienced people to work there. I was a bit shocked as I hadn't recovered from the fact of leaving the west and the life I had out there. I did miss Randy and the family of friends I had created out there. I did know for sure that I was to leave this area; my entire essence was telling me that and that was exactly what I had to do. I had followed my intuition and left that life behind because it wasn't serving me well at all and I was not living my life from a place that felt good inside. So I turned to the owner and said, "Sure, I would love to work here." He went and got the schedule and within a few minutes, I had enough shifts to keep me busy.

It's always a strange feeling starting all over again and I know for a fact that change is good but it's a strange feeling when you are in transition of life or in the unknown. I now found myself driving from Burlington to Mississauga; I was living in the city and travelling a highway. This was a big change as I just had spent four years surrounded by the most beautiful mountains and only travelling the highway when it was time for a trip to the city. I loved living in Banff and I am thankful for the love I did feel there and for the people that touched my life. I was now onto another new and exciting chapter and we know we are always in the correct spot at the correct time. This was where I was to be now at this time of my life.

It did take a bit to get comfortable with the size of this restaurant as it was extremely large. It was 7,000 square feet, the biggest restaurant I had ever worked in and I did love the restaurant business. The menu was big as well and the food was good. I was used to one chef and now, there were six cooks back there as when we got busy the kitchen got slammed. They did a good job but it was stressful for all of us. The owner was helping the guys on the line and he did create some extra tension as he really wasn't good with the stress of the restaurant business. I, on the other hand, had always loved the thrill of the rush time of the restaurant business. It was as if it was in my blood. My friend Jean was the same; she also loved the restaurant business and it's a business you either love or hate. I also love people, all people, the customers and the staff.

It was a few months later that Jean, I and friends that had met in Banff booked a fun weekend away in Collingwood. The owner of our restaurant decided to join us for the night. I, at this time, had no idea why he would be joining our group. As he arrived, all seemed good and we were all enjoying the night. I then went down to the bathroom and he followed me. Everything changed for us that night and a relationship began.

As the next few months passed, we then found that we were running this restaurant together. We actually did a good job and made a good team. My calmness and positivity was a good mix for my ex-partner uneasiness and negativity that was within him. I now realise he learned this from his childhood environment. The restaurant was going well at this moment in time and our relationship continued to grow. There was some judgment as the belief system which is programmed into us did come to the surface. Once again, we are all on our own journeys and it's no one's business or opinion who someone is going to love or wants to be in a relationship with. I can see this same issue right now between Andrew and me, everyone has an opinion of judgment upon our relationship. This has been a problem over time and mankind has not evolved at all. We have stayed in our ego and, therefore, we still prevent love from happening because it's not what we think it should look like. Maybe that's what Andrew and I are to teach people, love comes in ways you would never expect!

In time, we sold the restaurants and moved north and I ended up buying a small deli. My ex-partner found a good job at a local Marina which he always wanted to do. I was extremely happy being back in the restaurant business and my ex was extremely happy being out of the restaurant business. The greatest part of this change was that we both were now home every night for our kids so what happened to us ended up being the best thing for our family. Of course both of us thought this would be the worst thing. I was in fear for the outcome and it ended up being the better for our family to sell our business and move up north. I am also, right at this moment in time, experiencing the same exact thing. Interesting I opened up my computer and was editing this particular chapter and there are no coincidences. This has strengthened my faith in God, me and the universe.

Time did pass and I do believe due to the difference in our souls, me being more positive and wanting to live outside of the box and my ex being more negative and being programmed to live in the box, we started to grow apart in our marriage. He always said to me I was a dreamer and that I didn't see the reality of life. The problem was I just didn't want to accept or live in his reality or the way he thought life should be. Our soul's knowledge and belief systems were just too different. It was tough as I didn't want to lose my family and I loved him very much but I would have died inside if I would have stayed in that relationship. I now understand why we were both so unhappy as our emotional needs were not being met and our belief systems were just not compatible. All this combined was the reason for the breakup of our marriage.

It really was difficult to go through, as there was love but we didn't have the intimacy that we needed within the connection of our souls for our relationship to survive. Even though I do believe our paths were to cross and we were to have the two beautiful children together and promote growth within both of us. A lot of forgiveness has taken place and a lot of letting go. There is just no reason to hang onto the past, he is happy and I am happy. Our kids, extended kids and friends enjoy a happy environment at functions that we are all together at. This is the best part. I have totally accepted that the past was to unfold the way it did because it did and I have let it go. I am living in the present or the now and enjoying it. I don't have any love for my ex-partner and I don't have any hate as well. We have children together so there will always be a bond. We are friends and this is good for all of us involved. I am thankful I knew to heal and to read many books and attend retreats to become whole again.

Christmas

I had plans to travel to California again for the Christmas season. I was excited to see both my daughters and granddaughter. Brandon asked me if I wanted to attend a performance of his before I left. I was, of course, ecstatic about the invitation. He was to play at the senior's association located in beautiful Balm Beach. I had taken my mom there at few times to play cards therefore I was familiar with the location.

It was a cold clear night. As I arrived, I entered the building and sat down beside Brandon. I had taken him to over 300 performances so sitting beside him was natural for me. As I watched him, the first thing that came to mind was how very proud I was of him. He was such a beautiful young man inside and out. The people just loved him and enjoyed his talent.

I offered to get us a beer and approached the small bar area. The bartender started to get our beers but was stopped by a woman with authority. She then turned to me and said, "This is a private function and you are not allowed here."

I replied, "I am with Brandon and the beers are for us." She then went and spoke with Brandon. I'm not exactly sure what he said but the energy had changed dramatically when she returned. She smiled at me and said, "It's very nice to meet you and we really love Brandon."

I replied, "Thank you and yes, he is wonderful." I smiled at Brandon as I hand him a cold beer. Then I settled down to enjoy the show.

We had a great time. I enjoyed being close to Brandon and watching him perform. Then we went to see Lori for a quick visit as she was at work. We then jumped into a cab van with a few other friends heading down to the bar. I was sitting right by the sliding door and was to be the first person to get out of the cab. We pulled up, I opened the door and there was Andrew standing right in front of me. I got out of the cab and stood beside him. I could tell right away that he was in trouble. Everyone else got out of the van. Brandon said, "I'm going in the bar and I'll see you inside." I just smiled at Brandon.

Now Brandon was extremely supportive of my relationship with Andrew at the beginning. He was happy for me to be happy but as time progressed, he wanted more for me and wanted me to be valued and respected in a relationship. I turned to Andrew and I knew he was drunk. He was also cold as he had no coat on. I asked him if he was okay and he said, "No, they just kicked me out of the bar, said I had said something offensive to a customer." I didn't really say much I just stood there beside him. Other people were talking to him and one of the bouncers I knew came over. Andrew was shaking because he was cold and I asked the bouncer if he knew where Andrew's coat was. He said, "Yes, I will go and get it for you."

I was in a difficult situation for because this was my night with Brandon but I knew Andrew needed my help. I asked Andrew if he wanted me to take him home and he said, "Yes." The manager, at the time, showed up with the coat and I told Andrew I had to go and tell Brandon I was leaving. I went into the bar, found Brandon and explained I had to leave. He understood but there was disappointment in his eyes. I wasn't sure if it was because I was leaving or that I was going with Andrew.

Andrew and I were in a cab on our way to my house. We entered my house and I got us both a beer. Andrew then started to catch me up in his life. He told me that he was drinking a lot and his boss was going to fire him so he stopped drinking. Then he said, "I was doing great for three weeks and then I started drinking again and that was a couple weeks ago." He then went on to talk about what had happened to him as a kid, the abuse he had taken from his dad and others. He was a mess. I just listened and kept hugging him. I wanted to take all this pain away from Andrew, he had so much to heal; he was such a damaged soul. I knew in my heart that it would take time, patience and Andrew would have to want to heal and do the work. All I could do was be there for him, give him awareness and pray for him.

He then informed me that he had to move February 1st. I didn't say too much about him moving. We did end up having a romantic night as the connection never changes.

Andrew had returned into my life again. He was once again at my house often. We were playing cards, having fun and enjoying being together. During these times, there was no age difference. We were just two people having a good time just being together. We got along so well and the relationship felt so right. Time was getting closer to Andrew having to move so I offered if he was really stuck, he could rent a room from me.

It was three weeks later and Andrew asked to take the extra room from me. He said, "We can have sex every other day and twice on

Sundays." I knew to let life unfold but I was in an awe that this could be happening. I loved him so and I was happy for all of it.

It was February 1st. and Andrew was moving in. He didn't have much to move and he settled in quickly. I must say it was a strange feeling with Andrew moving in and I was having faith that this was unfolding for a reason.

It was within a couple days that I noticed a distance with Andrew. It was a strange feeling as when he was at my house in the past; I was able to love him all the time. Now I had to respect him differently as he was a paying roommate.

A week later, we were together playing cards and I got a little romantic and it was at this moment that the coldness was apparent from Andrew. It was like our sexual relationship was over. He didn't want to have sex with me anymore. My intuition was that the judgment of the world had got to him again or someone's specific judgment had got to him. Or maybe he just didn't want to hurt me. It was now like we were on a separation time again but now he was living in my house. I was now going through a very difficult time. I wondered if Andrew could hear me crying through the wall between us. I, at times, would text him telling him I was upset from one room to another and he would reply with 'please don't be upset'.

I also knew that I created this situation as I offered for Andrew to live in my house. He did come home every night and he continued to drink heavily. I did have a few conversations with God that weren't so nice as this was a very difficult time for me. I also did, at times, think to myself do I really want Andrew and all that comes with him? I then started to become more independent and then Andrew was gone for a few weekends. I felt as if he had met someone else again. Let me tell you the pain of it all was extremely overwhelming. It took a lot of strength but I was able to gather my ability to be my best during trouble times once again.

Then the bottom fell out of my life as something very bad happened to my daughter and granddaughter. Now all of a sudden everything stopped and nothing mattered to me and Andrew was by my side supporting me. He would just sit beside me at the bar and hold space for me. He would listen to me and play cards with me. He was there for me. Somehow I managed to get through this difficult time without losing myself. I was extremely thankful for my faith, as faith got all of us through it.

It was a few months later that Andrew ended up back in my bed. I feel he just couldn't deny his true feelings any longer. Our relationship would go a few months as if we were married and then it would change again. It was very difficult at times and great other times. During these times I was helping Andrew with getting his life going with a birth certificate and bank account.

Things then changed at work for Andrew as well and he was now unemployed. He was a good worker and great at his job but now I was helping him by keeping a roof over his head, food on the table and beer in his belly. It was unconditional love that I had for Andrew. I loved him so. Our relationship was also developing into a constant for both of us.

It's a Spiritual Connection

Well, all the pieces starting to come together. It's finally starting to make sense. Why the very first time Andrew saw me, he had a connection with me that he had to ask Brandon who I was. Why he sat beside me for a year straight, why the connection was so passionate and why the intimacy was so strong. It's an awaking for both of us in the relationship realm and it's a spiritual connection and one from the soul. It's a twin flame connection, a connection that is a one of a kind. I do believe when this happens, it will be when you are least expecting it and with someone you least expect this could happen with. The draw is so strong that you will know it's something different as it's one of the most powerful feelings I have ever felt. This is like the story of Adam and Eve, they were one soul in the beginning, their soul was split creating a spiritual connection. When this connection is found or these two souls that are from the same cell unit connect, it is like two magnets coming together. I couldn't understand it in the beginning why I felt such a pull towards Andrew. I have never felt anything like that in my entire life and I get it now as it's a spiritual connection, a connection from the soul. Also a past life connection and when our souls are connected, look out as truly that's what we are to connect with on earth.

Passion

Before my friendship fell away from Sue, I can remember saying to her that I had fallen in love with Andrew and how did that happen? I was even outside the bar trying to kiss Andrew and wondering myself what had happened to me. Obviously my soul was finally alive and ready to love and the passion that had been bottled up in me was now pouring out of me. This passion was more that I could have imagined. I also believe this passion is something that we all have within us and we are keeping bottled up. The passion I have within was hidden and not surfacing because I had pushed it down so far in my awareness. Then once it came to the surface, it was so strong that I didn't understand what was happening to me. Yes, this going from one extreme to the other was difficult to understand. I don't think it matters that I am a woman; we all have this passion within us. Although we as women are ready to love more easily and we as females are more connected to our souls, that's why we are to give birth to the children. All children have to go through the woman to exist. That was designed for a reason.

Men are trained from centuries ago to control their emotions and feelings as they are the providers and the hunters. This is another belief that is passed down that doesn't serve us the people at all in any way. I wish I could talk to Andrew and explain that our relationship is more of a spiritual connection. I am now coming to the awareness to be thankful to God for sending me this amazing connection and igniting the fire in my soul.

This is a very deep spiritual connection and causes you to awaken everything within you. When you connect to your twin flame in a spiritual way, you create a huge energy in the world. It's like you are bringing a bit of heaven and earth together or bringing heaven to earth and this is very powerful. This also makes perfect sense as this is what happened between Andrew and me. Even when we are just standing beside each other, this causes more awaking within the people of the world. Awe, the power of love!

Also our union creates growth within the people around us. From my children to the people Andrew works with to everyone else. Wow, how amazing is that.

On our journey, both Andrew and mine, we both wanted more in our lives. We wanted a spiritual connection or a loving connection from the heart and that's exactly what we got. It's so powerful within that it creates light that shines a light on all our darkness which needed to heal within the two of us. Yes, right now we are healing all the darkness, fears and doubt within us. Now this process could take some time because there are a lot of beliefs between us and healing that we both have to do but when that is complete, we will have the most powerful union of two people. Our souls were split many, many years ago and when they reunite together, it will be very powerful, it will be heaven on earth.

They also say this union pushes us to heal; it pushes Andrew and me to heal separately and together and exposes all our deepest secrets and past pains. These pains could even have been carried over from a past lifetime as I do believe we are both very old souls and our souls have for sure met before. All this relationship turmoil is now happening so we can heal what needs to heal within us to have total consciousness within our relationship. This is the reason for a twin flame relationship. This understanding helps a bit when dealing with the incredible pain that comes with it. Andrew and I are to be in complete consciousness together so we can set the example and be true love and light. I don't believe there are too many couples that have such a connection, a true connection or a relationship without ego. I know it's rare!

Andrew and I will be a relationship like this once we are done our healing and we are valuing our connection. We are both being tested in a very large way first because of the age difference. It's a huge age difference and even harder because I, the woman, am older. I also know it's much harder for him. We have been programmed that the man is to be older than the women in a love relationship. Therefore, Andrew has a huge belief to let go of.

We are also from two complete different worlds, almost similar to Jack and Rose from Titanic. I deal with a lot of judgment with the belief that the man should have more than the woman and that he should look after the woman. "You deserve more, Jan," I have heard that a lot but I don't care about material things. I do care about a relationship full of love and consciousness. I know for sure that when we are finished all our healings, we will teach others to value love from the soul and bring God and heaven to earth. Love will prevail no matter what and there will be no stopping us, this I know as truth.

At this moment in time, I just have to continue to work on myself and write this book. It happens to be that it is going to rain for the next four days and I feel that is a direct message for me to pay attention to write and write some more.

The Baseball Game

Andrew and I decided to attend a baseball game in Toronto. It had been a while since I had gone to the city. Andrew loved all sports and I enjoyed them as well. Andrew had fun picking the seats and we were all set to go for the day. I love to drive but I don't really know the city that well. I was thankful Andrew grew up in Toronto and knew his way around.

We arrived early and parked right close to the stadium. We then needed a beer so we started walking around to find a place we both liked. Andrew and I had the same interests and enjoyed the same things; this was nice.

We first found an upper class outdoor patio. I noticed a little judgment as we approached the bar and I wasn't sure if it was about the age difference or the clothes we were wearing. We had Blue Jays t-shirts and shorts on comfortable and fan-like but maybe not high class enough. We had one beer, looked at the menu and moved to another restaurant.

Things were much different in this place; there was no judgement at all. It was more of a middle class restaurant and the energy was friendly. We also connected with a family sitting at the bar. They were my age and there was no judgment. They loved Andrew as Andrew is fun to be around. He was outgoing, funny and sincere. I did love sitting with him and just being around him. It felt so normal, real and home for me.

We then checked out one more bar, got street food, which was the best sausage on a bun I had ever had, and then head to find our gate of entrance. Andrew had the tickets and I was just a bit in front of him and I went into the main Gate 6 line. Andrew didn't follow me and he went into Gate 5 line. I looked at him and said, "This line is fine we can get in this way."

He replied, "No, it says this is our gate and this is the correct line."

I once again say, "I think this line is good."

Andrew says, "Listen, Linda, I think we should be in this line." Well, I started to laugh. Have you seen the kid on YouTube that talks to his mother saying, "Listen Linda?" Well, it's pretty funny and Andrew sounded just like this. At this moment, Andrew and I both noticed there are four women listening and watching us. They were also laughing with us. I then smiled at Andrew and joined him in his line. He was also smiling and laughing. It was like we were an old married couple in love. This was a moment that I started to see the joy our bond and relationship brought to others.

We then entered, got some more beer and found our seats. Andrew once again became the life of the party. Everyone around us enjoyed him so much. We had a great time. As we were walking towards the car, there was a group of people dancing to the song, *Uptown Funk,* and I joined in. I loved this song and I loved to dance. It was a beautiful moment for me as Andrew just stopped and smiled at me. He had no judgment or was in no hurry. He let me be me and loved to see me having fun. When I was finished, we continued to walk to the car. We got some more street food and then decided to go on a tour of where Andrew had grown up. I was a little concerned about it bringing up past pain but I said, "Sure we can go and see where you grew up."

Andrew knew the city well and soon we were on the street he had spent his childhood. He was so proud of the area and happy to be seeing it again. I noticed as we slowly passed the house he grew up in, some pain returned. It was plain to see on his face. I just kept being loving and supportive. He talked about his dad and he was focusing on the positive he had experienced.

Next we passed the neighbour's house, this being the house where not good things happened to Andrew. At this moment, both of us had tears in our eyes. There was silence for a second and Andrew said, "My dad didn't believe me." I just looked at Andrew with heartfelt eyes. He then said, "He just kept sending me back there."

I then replied, "I am so sorry that happened to you. You were an innocent child and you didn't deserve for that to happen to you." There were more tears running down Andrew's face. I also said, "People were not aware of the high level of sexual abuse happening to children like we do now. It doesn't make it any easier and I am sorry that happened to you, Andrew."

Andrew said, "He didn't believe me."

I replied, "That is the dysfunction that happened years ago, people swept child abuse under the carpet and tried to hide it. This has been happening for many years. Your dad didn't know how to deal with it."

There was silence for a few minutes. All I could think about was that I didn't care about what had happened to Andrew when he was a young boy. It didn't change how much I loved him. It actually made me want to love him more.

We then tried to find some family that owned a bar in the area but it was closed. It was then time to head up the highway home. We had had a fantastic day full of great times. When Andrew and I are together away from Middletown, we always have a great time.

The Ego

I am starting to understand the true meaning of the concept of mind control which creates our ego. We are a society that is so driven by the ego and we are programmed that way. This is why the consciousness of the world is so very low and we, as humans, are in such bad shape. I could barely sleep last night and I am in a bit of a funk with putting a lot of the puzzle pieces together. It's kind of scary but it makes so much sense. I have even had to leave work with my laptop to the nearest Tim Horton Coffee shop to write this chapter as this awareness is very important.

What I have learned is to follow the money and you will find the control of the programming to keep us in our egos. This is what the elite have done to us to keep us as slaves, in the box and to depopulate. First, they give us the belief that we are to go to work every day, at the same place, save our money and live in the same house for our entire life. And, of course, pay our taxes so they can continue the control they have on us. This is also why they encourage no gender and to limit the family. Their real agenda is to keep us as slave and away from our natural spirituality. It's really good vs evil and its God vs Satan, and it's very simple and right in our faces. Moreover, it has been like that for a very long time on earth.

I go back to love the enemy and that's hard to do when you realise what the enemy is really up to. Look at the love relationships that don't make it because of the ego. Look at how many unhealthy relationships there are and how many families are not together. They have even taken the Lord's Prayer out of our schools to limit our knowledge of God and they have and are doing whatever they can to keep love apart. We, the slaves, are walking around in zombie mode. I can see them on their yachts laughing at mankind, slapping each other on the back saying, "Good job done." The darkness is in so much control and we, the people, have to wake up to this awareness.

They keep us in the games of the ego in love relationships and it's almost impossible to get past the games of the ego, especially jealousy. I have lived my entire life surrounded by jealousy and it has got to stop.

When can we ever break this cycle and be happy for one another? Can we understand when someone is doing great or experiencing love that we don't want to stop it that we want to stand in the light of love. If your girlfriend is falling in love with someone or is in love with someone, don't feel bad for yourself because you are alone or haven't found your soulmate or twin flame, yet be happy for someone else. This will happen to you when you are ready and it's your turn. Be happy that someone close to you is experiencing love and is experiencing a bit of heaven on earth, as this is our entire purpose as mankind. We are to remember this as this is where we come from and it's our worst worry when we do reincarnate. Yes, we worry that we are not going to remember the power of love and what our purpose is here on earth. This is important because our purpose on earth is the same, we are to create heaven on earth and experience spiritual growth, and it's plain and simple. We are to do this in our own lives no matter how different they are. This is why we have spiritual teachers and spiritual leaders; they have remembered this knowledge and are trying to wake the rest of mankind up. There are a few that chose to do this as their destiny on earth, and I believe I am one of them. My consciousness level is getting very high and I am becoming stronger and stronger out of the control of the matrix. Plus, it says in the Bible that God will always plant the seed of his knowledge on earth and this will always be apparent on earth. No matter how much control the darkness has or Satan has, he will never be able to wipe God out or the knowing of Jesus. I don't know how to explain the importance of understanding, the power of the ego and that the ego wants to be in control, and it's stopping us from having healthy lives. Here are a few of the games of the ego; living in the story, judgment, blame, victim mode, jealousy and acting from woundedness.

And it's not all our fault. We are being programmed to stay in the mind and not to hear our souls. They hypnotise us through the news, newspapers, CNN, chemtrails, music, chemicals in our foods, vaccines, the TV and movies too. They inundate us with FEAR constantly. We have to wake up to this, be aware of what is really going on so we can take back our lives and our dreams.

I do believe that the only way to break the cycle or break the control they have on us is through spirituality, controlling our thoughts (as we have sixty thousand a day) and emotions and love! Connecting or finding spirituality and living your life from this place is living your life in and from a place of LOVE. This is the only way to make a change in the world. It's not an easy thing as the body is self-programmed to experience the emotions of fear and we become addicted to the emotion of fear. This can happen for different reasons. One being what trauma we experience in our lifetimes and also due to what beliefs we have taken on. I'm fortunate not to have had experienced too much trauma and, therefore, the work I had to do was easily obtainable. I still had a lot of work to do and obtainable in seven years. You might think this is a long time but it took me forty five years to acquire the need to heal therefore seven years is really a small amount of time to heal. On the other hand, I have so much compassion for Andrew at this moment as he has experienced great trauma. I also see what LOVE did for Christine and Brandon. The power of love broke the ego and brought them back in touch with their souls and they are both leading healthy lives.

Christine is now raising three beautiful children from a place of love. Although these children are dealing with vaccines, chemicals in their foods, the TV and music, they are in a healthy family life, spending many hours together. They are also fishing, collecting rocks, and swimming while being surrounded by the love of family. They are so blessed to have such love all around them. This will keep them on the correct path, away from drugs and help them find their destiny.

Now Brandon was able to heal and find his destiny with the power of love. I know that this is the greatest gift I will have ever given him, this being the gift of LOVE. I know he may not at this time realise how important our bond is but he's young and I do know that he understands it more and more as he matures. This love or the power of it now lies within his subconscious as well. He has the knowing that I am always behind him and that I will never leave him and that I love him with all my heart. I do believe it's one of the most powerful gifts you can receive from anyone.

With Andrew, I believe the love I gave him helped him as he was totally disconnected with his soul. He was living life from a very bad place and numbing every second he could. He had a lot of knowledge of what was going on in the world, a lot of common sense and he was smart but he was living in his past pain and unable to break the control of the ego. Andrew also has one of the most beautiful souls and this is why I love him and why I connected with him. Truly, it was the power of love that helped him wake up and take control of his life. The power of love connected him back to his soul. He woke up and now he is getting his life together.

I have said to Brandon over and over again for the past six years that it's all about the power of love and I didn't even realise that depth to that statement as I do now. I knew it was truth and the power of love breaks the hypnotism that has been placed upon us humans.

They also want to control the bloodlines and one way is through vaccines. The mercury they put in these vaccines is deadly. If they could control us with the microchip, they would have already but interestingly, negative blood people will reject all and any foreign objects, especially the mark of the beast. This is God evidence that he exists with the negative bloodline and especially O negative blood. They say that O negative blood is the bloodline of the Holy Grail and this means that people with this bloodline have the knowledge of God and the heavens within. O negative blood is unique as people with this bloodline are able to give their blood to everyone but they can only receive O negative blood. I have O negative blood. I do know a very few that have O negative blood as it's rare. I have read that O negative blood has the knowledge of God and heaven within this bloodline, as this is why Jesus wanted the disciples to drink his blood at the last supper so they could have his knowledge.

I have also met some people that have O negative blood and they are still in their egos and have not yet connected with this knowledge within. I do believe because they have not found self-love or are living without love in their lives; this keeps them in their ego or disserving beliefs. It is the power of self-love within that is so very important to create or tap into as well. We have to make these changes for our children and our grandchildren. It's really quite simple, God gives us lots of signs that He exists and we need to pay attention to it.

Therefore stop watching the news, stop reading the newspaper and watching those horrible movies. Listen to the good music and dance often. Follow the 10 commandments and be kind to everyone. Most of all, stay in the state of LOVE! Understand the games of the ego and shut them down. It's all right and good to feel what you are feeling and be open to this with your partner and transforms this into strength of how you are feeling not a weakness. As Pitbull says, "I took a negative to a positive and look at my life now." We have to have the negatives and the darkness so we can see the light, we just don't have to have it rule the world. We would have so much abundance if we would eliminate the greed and the corruption. The world is big enough for all of us if we just followed God's message.

Update

Andrew has now lived with me for nine months. We have had some good times and some bad times. We have stayed up until early hours of the morning playing cards and drinking. We have celebrated Brandon's marriage to Lori and Andrew was close and respectful during this time. This being the first wedding he had attended. My daughter Emily was home for the wedding, which was a blessing for me.

It is now the end of October and I am set for another trip to California. Unfortunately, things are not good at all with Andrew and me. It was his birthday at the beginning of the month. I was very giving and by his side until a young woman joined us and his attention was on her. Of course, at this moment, I felt very used and betrayed. We had words outside and he said to me, "I don't want to be with you."

I said, "Fine, you could have told me earlier." I left the bar extremely upset but I knew this was the best thing for me once again. Now, really how many times did I have to go through the same thing and have egg thrown on my face? I guess that had to happen once again because it was happening.

Although, I had had enough of the life style we were living. I had completely gone down to Andrew's lifestyle and it was consuming me. I also was short on cash as I spent a lot of money on Andrew. It was what I did for love and unconditional love but I was losing my self-love or what I had started to develop for myself. I guess I needed more lessons and I was not ready to wake up to this as this is what was happening to me.

Andrew did arrive home the next day still drunk, telling me he had been up all night. He did look as if this had taken place. Interesting enough, he was very sorry for what he had said and we ended up in the bedroom for many hours. The next morning, I thought to myself why didn't he have sex with this young beautiful girl? Why was he with me?

While I was in California, I had the awareness I had to get away from Andrew. I wasn't happy at all in the life I was living with him. I also knew it was only me that had created this lifestyle as I am the creator of my reality. I knew, at this time, that I had to get him out of my house. I arrived home and the opportunity showed itself. I had heard that Andrew had had people over as one of the girls stopped by to visit my other roommate. I received two different stories from my roommates and I chose not to believe Andrew. Then he came home very, very drunk and was obnoxious and verbally out of control. We fought in the living room and the dysfunction of Andrew was the worse I had ever seen or really imagined was inside of him. I then went to bed and he left at 5 am.

The next morning, I was a mess and I knew I had to do something, as I was now fearful in my own home. Andrew had reconnected with an old friend, a guy he had known for many years. He was spending a lot of time with him so I packed up all his things and left them on his friend's doorstep. I texted Andrew and told him as no one was home, knowing they were together. He owed me money and what he had lost for paid rent lost and he was still up a few hundred dollars. He was angry with me but I reinforced the fact that he was so drunk and verbally abusive in my home. There was silence and then acceptance. As he returned back the key to my other roommate, he said, "I guess I went too far."

Time Heals

I do believe that this is a true statement or belief and I do believe that it does serve us well. I also know that you have to do the work when you are healing; this is always on going and part of life.

Time has passed and I have healed. I am thankful for the learning and growth that I have experienced with my time with Andrew. I do not, at this time, feel that there is much of a chance that we will reunite in this lifetime. I also don't know if he will be able to sustain the growth and light that he experienced, as I am not sure if he is doing the work or really got any of it. I have been following my motto and what I know works for me and it is to 'Let GO', 'Have Faith' and 'Pay Attention'. I know the correct path will always be shown if we let it and if we are open to seeing it.

I did see Andrew on the street and when our eyes met, I could see the pain in him and he waved at me. I smiled back at him and my heart felt like a lightning bolt had hit and then a couple tears popped out of my eyes. These tears also felt like past pain tears and as if I had been here before.

Later this day, I heard a strange thing on the radio. They were talking about people that were getting married to themselves. My first reaction was that is sad but as I continued to listen to what they had to say, it actually made sense. They talked about not wanting to be hurt anymore, not wanting to play the games that took place in some relationships and not wanting to give up being themselves or their life purpose. I could understand why mankind was starting to feel happy and okay being single and living alone.

Mankind has not figured out the importance of love and how to be in a loving, easy relationship, one from the soul. There is a lot of work to a relationship and there is pain that comes with this process but we are to grow and love during our lifetimes. If we were living our relationships from the soul, they would all be healthy relationships full of love.

Love

Love is the most powerful and strongest essence we have on earth. When valued and used in a positive way, it can move mountains and make anything happen. Jesus was able in time and when doing the work to become a true essence of love and therefore he was able to move mountains and manifest whatever he wanted to. We have to remember God is love and living from the soul is love. Living from the ego is FEAR!

We are born as essences of love but things change as we adapt to the programming of society. The beliefs and the judgments of others are taught to us. We, as children, are programmed to be the way they think we should be. We are programmed in our conscious and our subconscious in our first seven years of life. We have to reprogram our conscious with the awareness of the games of the ego and we may also have to reprogram our subconscious as well. It is our subconscious that makes ninety-five percent of our decisions and it makes decisions like a computer program.

In our youth, we also experience traumatic situations that are forced upon us, which darkens and fades the love we have within for the world and ourselves. We may find, as adults, that we have to heal what has happened to us as children and regain the love we have within our souls to find our destiny or the life we deserve. I do believe that love and the ability to live from our souls fades as we develop in our lives. I also know you can heal this and find the amazing strength and love the lies inside of you.

You can do this by reading self-help books, by monitoring your thoughts, being aware of your emotions with learning to control them and releasing the addiction to your emotions, Ever wonder why every two or three weeks you get angry or jealous? Many people are addicted to their emotions. Getting angry can be the fix the body gets accustomed to and needs just like a shot of rye or a shot of heroine.

More Relationships

I had a friend, who's in her early sixty, attractive and fit, tell me recently that when she met a new guy, she would have sex with him right away, thinking this would keep him but this was the opposite to how it unfolded. This woman and I have been friends for a few years now and she was able to be open with me with her personal life as she knew I was non-judgmental. She then explained this type of thinking or belief also left her self-worth very low.

She really enjoyed hearing that Andrew and I sat beside each other for an entire year before we had sex. I do believe hearing this changed her belief on this topic. She also loves the idea that he is much younger than me and that has opened many doors as she is now letting life unfold with no preconceived age agenda in place. I told her that being with someone younger is great and difficult at the same time. I would prefer 10 years age difference as I am still working on releasing this belief. I then reinforced to her how we can take on a belief that can be disserving and to have awareness around her beliefs. The best outcome of our conversation was she is now going to start a friendship with a patience partner before a sexual relationship occurs, which is beautiful to hear. Plus, she deserves this as a solid relationships, and anything solid starts with a foundation.

I do still miss Andrew at times and I will always love him but I had to save myself and I want someone to be constant in my life as we know what lack of consistency can do to oneself. I have complete faith that this will happen. I am thankful for the time with Andrew, as it was beautiful but I want and deserve more. I know that this love will take time to fade away or maybe it never will. I know that when the connection is strong and possibly a past life connection, and twin flame connection there are unseen cords between you and this person. I was told once that Andrew and I had a rainbow between us. I felt this was true and I could almost feel this connection. I trust in life and know it will unfold; faith is all I need and have at this moment.

I also know this separation is a good thing for Andrew as he is still finding his way and discovering what he wants in his life. This is his journey and his path. I do pray for him to get out of the bar one day and to want more for himself. He has so much wisdom in him, he never misses a thing and once he connects with that, it will be a wonderful thing.

I would never be where I am today if I hadn't had the connections with all of the men in my life, some good and some not so good. Some of them made me feel loved and some of them hurt me to the core. I did experience pain but they all gave me tremendous inner growth. I know right now I would never accept an unhealthy relationship or settle for anything that wasn't good for me in any relationship. This being from the clerk at the grocery store or the next man I marry, as every person you meet you have a relationship with.

I am thankful for each and everyone one of these men, as it was a combo effort getting to the place that I am. I needed the connection from each of them alongside the inner strength I had within to get myself to this wonderful place, which is connected to my higher self. Thine is the kingdom we know that but God wants us to learn from each other. This I also know to be true, so that person who has caused you so much pain and then growth, forgive them for you and only you. Know inside that you had to experience that connection and relationship to get to where you are today.

Time to Move Forward

There is always a song, there is just always a song and right now it is, *I Want Something Just Like This*. I love the line, "I want someone to kiss and someone to miss." Of course that means someone to love because you want to kiss and miss someone you love. I think that's what the entire human race is looking for. We are essences of love and we are to find love on earth. Therefore, we need to wake up and value love when we find it! It's as simple as that!

I had the pleasure because it is always a pleasure to sit and talk to Steve yesterday at work. Funny thing, we can talk for two hours and it goes by quickly. He often reminds me of my dad as my dad was a kind man and one people loved to talk to. I did love my dad very much and I know he is always with me.

Steve and I would talk about everything and everyone. He would ask me how Andrew was and I would smile and explain okay but that we are apart at the moment. He would smile at me as he knew I loved Andrew and understood how hard that was for me.

Steve would talk about the women in his life as his beloved wife of fifty-two years of marriage who passed away suddenly. There was no judgement from either of us and this was the beauty of our relationship. He was a good-looking man for 76 and he did offer to date me but there was no spark. I knew there would only be a platonic relationship and this was beautiful in its self. The most amazing thing about Steve was that he believed in me. He believed and felt that I was connected to God and that I have a strong healing ability within. This was nice as he was a very successful man. It felt good hearing that he saw my strengths and my light within.

I had worked with him a lot with the sudden passing of his wife. He explained that his religious beliefs were that you could not date for a year to let the soul of the person that passes be at rest. I knew that there was some transition for a soul on the other side but most were okay quite soon because they were on the other side. I also thought this year was good for Steve's soul as it needed the healing. He then talked about not being the greatest partner and was God punishing him for this? I explained, no, that it was his wife's time to go and it had nothing to do with him. He also felt that he should have treated her better when she was alive and said, "I never thought she would leave me."

I then said, "This is a very wonderful awareness for you and I believe it will be valuable in another relationship to come." I could see the relief on his face and throughout his body. I listened to Steve often and this was from the heart.

A few months later, Steve said to me, "Jan, you are the real deal and you should have a church." Now Steve had mentioned this before and I wasn't too sure about it at first, as I had a limited or preconceived view that I would be a writer and a film director. Although I know I can still write books, screenplays and have a church at the same time.

Therefore, this time, I looked at him strangely and said, "Yes you are correct, I should have a church." I could see the pleased look on Steve's face and we both felt warmth within.

I believe the teachings of God and Jesus are the only way to survive in this world in a happy and healthy way. This is true but the deliveries of these teachings have not evolved with mankind. Steve's already started two churches and they are still reciting scripture from two thousand years ago. Plus, the Catholic Church has come so far away from the teachings of God that it's actually hard to believe they have evolved this way. My first little blue book contains the teachings of God, *A Woman's Passage to Freedom.* This message is delivered in a simple easy fashion for everyone to understand in the 21st century. Plus, I would be honoured to have a church to help the people. I even had a vision of a full church with me, giving heartfelt sermons that people understand. These people are lining up for healings with me giving them a small cross to take home with them to keep the light of God close at all times. I also could see us feeding the people. I knew this was possible as Steve told me he already had built two churches in his lifetime. This would be number three and this would be wonderful.

Interestingly enough, Steve did enter into another relationship and he, at first, repeated the same patterns with his deceased wife. He would say, "I haven't been so nice and I am controlling at times." I would explain to him that control is not good for anything and it usually back fires in a relationship. Control is also a game of the ego and ego means to edge God out! Steve would listen and agree. He was able to change his behaviour even at the age of 76 and the relationship continued to grow.

I did change jobs a year later. I did hear from Steve a few times at the beginning but I haven't heard from him lately. I feel he is doing well and his new relationship is intact.

Healthy Relationships

I now reflect to my life at this moment in time and I only have healthy relationships in my life. I must say I have come a long way! I first look to my children and yes, I am thankful they have matured and are in their middle twenties and I am past the difficult times, as there were a few difficult and trying times and we have the most amazing relationships. I have now learned to let them go and let them grow. I have also learned to set my boundaries and always be my authentic self. This being a major key and crucial combination and it's great to see that not one of them would expect anything different from me and this is the best. If you can be you without any anger and just be and say what you want and what you believe in as long as it is from a conscious state, you are okay. Therefore, all of my four children are good and three of them have partners in their lives and I love and accept all of them. I could get involved in a couple situations but I have learned to sit back, as it's, once again, their journey. It's their choices and their lessons to create the growth within that they all need. Remember there are no coincidences so whatever is happening to people around you is happening to them for a reason. I do believe if I thought there was a safety issue for my kids or my grandkids, I would have to say something but for now it is totally their journeys. This is the most amazing place to be and I highly recommend it.

My parents have both passed to heaven, therefore I can't really comment on a living parental relationship but I can tell you I have peace with both their spirits. There are no regrets and no pain within my memories with them. I did what I had to do from a place of integrity and that is the best you can do with elderly parents.

If your relationship was not good with your parents when they were alive, you can still make peace with their spirits and I do believe their spirit will want to make peace with you. I know this might sound strange but it's the truth. You can talk to them as you can to any spirit and they will listen. The energy will change around you and you will be able to see the peace on the outside and the inside of you. The spirits of our parents can stay with us throughout our lifetime.

Most of all, I have the understanding not to place any force on any part of my love relationship. It is actually perfect just the way it is and I was going to let it unfold that way. I checked a couple days later and I was still blocked from talking to Andrew and this felt just fine. Strangely, I was thankful for this because I didn't need to worry about where he was or if he was going to answer me or when I was going to see him again. I knew to keep going with my life and to have faith in this relationship that if it was meant to be, it was meant to be.

Interestingly enough, as soon as you have awareness or you are changing an old behaviour pattern that is no longer serving you, you are immediately tested in this area. This seems to be what happens to me and so the tests have begun.

I once again found myself experiencing fear and a low self-worth within towards my partner relationships. I knew that these were old beliefs around romantic relationships, or how I should or would have reacted previously when romantic relationships didn't work out or I found myself alone again. When this memory surfaced, I could hear my mind telling me to react and in not such a good way. I just let those thoughts come forward as you cannot stop a thought and then I replaced these thoughts with a question of 'Are you sure?' I then tried to feel from my heart instead, which brought me to more of a place of reality and more of what was truly going on not what my mind was trying to create. It took a bit of work and I was able to stay peaceful, non-reactive and increased my self-worth. Plus, if the situation of being alone again was going to unfold, then there was nothing I could do about it and I for sure had the knowing that something better would come forward as it always does.

I did well until the middle of the night and I found this unhealthy pattern of dealing with fear in a romantic relationship come forward again. I worked some more on releasing it and I was able to fall back a sleep and this morning I am okay. I once again thank Andrew for bringing me all these awareness and now all these tests. I am thankful to be releasing all these old patterns that have been passed on for many years and that have not been serving me very well at all. We are really in the darkness with relationships and finally I see the light.

The Miami Miracle

Andrew had now been out of the house and basically out of my life for three weeks and I was doing okay. I still missed him but I was getting stronger every day and praying to God all the time for strength and direction as I still deeply loved him. My prayers were answered and a strong message came from God and, of course, it was for both of us.

Andrew and my now only roommate Greg are big NFL fans, Greg being a Green Bay Packers fan, Andrew being a Pittsburgh fan and me being a Miami fan. The Miami Dolphins is my team. They were playing Sunday December 9th and I was unable to watch the game with Greg as I had a birthday party to attend that day. It was Tuesday morning that I connected with Greg and he said to me, "Jan, I have to show you something, they are calling it the Miami Miracle." I then stood behind Greg and was looking at his phone as he searched YouTube to find the video he was looking for. I noticed the video was titled 'The Miami Miracle' and I was stunned at this time. The video started to play and it was amazing. They were losing by five points and there were seven seconds on the clock and the play began. There was a fantastic pass and then two lateral passes, not one but two and then a 50-yard run for a touchdown and the announcer called it a "Miracle".

I said to Greg, "I have goose bumps."

He replied, "So do I." I watched this video a few times and then I asked Greg how Pittsburgh did and he told me they lost to the worst team.

I then started to put it all together and all I could say over and over again was, "I was the miracle in Andrew's life and he didn't see it and I am sure he was a miracle in my life too." What a sign from God, the angles, what a message. People and love in our lives are a miracle and do we see it and do we value it?

I prayed at this time that Andrew saw the Miami Miracle as this is a direct message from God to him. Our connection and our love was a miracle for both of us. Then I noticed the yardage for the touchdown was 69 yards; this meant to me intimacy, which Andrew and I had so much of. It was all there, we had it all. Then I remembered Andrew saying to me at the very beginning of our relationship that he asked for an older woman. Well, God heard him and gave him me and he didn't see it or value me at all.

Most of all, it was love and once again do we value love? I see many similar situations where the correct person has been placed into someone's life and they do not see the miracle of it. Love is a miracle, we don't see it very often and we do not value it. Unfortunately, we try to control it, we are jealous of it and we sometimes turn it into anger.

I can see God from up above saying. "I just sent you exactly what you were asking for in a partner and you did not see it, value it or respect it." And this day in December, God sent Andrew a message that I was his Miami Miracle and it was good for me to know I was a miracle in Andrew's life and he just didn't see it.

How many miracles does God send us that we don't see? I know now, many, there are many miracles and especially miracles of love that are not seen.

I challenge you now to look into your lives, especially the men and see all the miracles you have and all the miracles you have missed. Plus, love and relationships are miracles, miracles and proof of God!

An Other Woman

I sat at the bar where Andrew was working, enjoying a glass of wine with a girlfriend of mine talking to a new bartender. She was very personable and we were enjoying the conversation. A few minutes later, Andrew came out of the kitchen, glanced over at the bar area and returned to the kitchen. I then noticed the glazed look on the bartender's face. She for sure was smitten with Andrew. I first thought to God you have to be kidding. You are placing another young beautiful woman right in front of Andrew? I then wondered, was this connection there to keep distance between Andrew and me so that I would stay focused on my books, movies and my destiny? Or were there learnings for Andrew and for me too?

Friday night, I ended up back in the bar as Brandon was playing. I was feeling better as I wasn't drinking much and I was sleeping more. Plus, I didn't have to wake up wondering what time Andrew would be home and what shape he would be in. The most important thing was that I was writing and doing readings again. I had my life back as I so often gave it to Andrew. There was no blame, as first of all, blame is a manmade belief and truly blame doesn't exist. I gave my life and my power to Andrew often and with a smile on my face.

Andrew was closing the kitchen, so it was a while until he finished and came out of the kitchen. Firstly, I noticed a distance between him and this new woman bartender. As the night passed, I ended up surrounded by many men. I then noticed that Andrew slid into the seat beside this girl. I was surprised that it didn't hurt that much and I moved him out of my house, knowing someone else could walk into his life. And once again I had no choice as I had to save my life.

The night was unfolding and I was doing pretty well. Then Andrew passed me and I slightly touched his hand to talk to him. I wanted to tell him that I had bumped into his mother and that she was concerned about him. For Andrew, this would be important and his reaction was, "Don't touch me." I was quite surprised. Like, you didn't want me or valued me, you were always drunk and verbally abused so I am out of your life, therefore don't be upset with me. I then followed him out where he was standing with some people including the new woman and I said, "I just wanted to tell you I saw your mom the other day and we talked for quite a while." I then turned around and went back into the bar. They returned into the bar, walked by me, giving me a look as if I had the problem.

I then remembered I had donated a painting that was very special to me and it was hanging in the hallway towards the washroom. I knew I would get it back somehow so I went to Brandon and asked for his car keys which he gave to me immediately. I walked by all of them, took the painting and walked back by them with my painting in hand. I felt bitter coldness and deceit from this group. Andrew and I were going through a divorce and I was taking what was important to me.

About 30 mins later, everything had calmed down and we all were enjoying Brandon's music; this new woman in Andrew's life came up to me, grabbed me and said, "Let's go dance." Well, I knew not to and all of my body stopped and I said, "NO." She asked me why and I told her I had been involved with Andrew for a few years and I didn't want to be involved. She went on that she hoped it wouldn't interfere with our relationship and that she was in love with someone else and that she would never be involved with the kitchen staff. I then said that Andrew and I had a lot of great sex and she turned and walked away. This, at the time, I thought that was the end of it.

It was two weeks later that I Andrew told me I said to her to go and have fun with him. I said, "NO, I did not say that and I wouldn't say that ever." He actually came back at me a few days later saying that I did say exactly that and that there would be no reason why this new woman would lie to him.

I said, "You would believe her over me?" Unbelievable and, of course, there would be a reason she would lie.

Now I was totally engaged, my need to defend myself was in full form and I was now waiting for the time to get it straight or correct because for me, if someone lied about what I said, I needed to get the truth out.

It was five days later I went to have a drink at the bar and there was this woman working and asked me what I would like to drink. I said to her, "I am not sure what you think you heard but I said that we, as in Andrew I, and had a lot of great sex."

She replied, "And I walked away."

I said, "Yes, you did."

She then said, "I hopped Andrew is not pitting both of us at each other." Then I asked for a beer, a Corona.

I then texted Jennifer and she replied she would be right over. I was so thankful for her and glad she was coming because the anger I was feeling and the need to defend and engage was overwhelming. They were lucky my energy didn't knock out their computer system or shatter a few windows because I was upset.

Jennifer arrived and this new woman was pleasant to her. Then Andrew arrived and this new girl went to him immediately and they were having a heated conversation and then Andrew gave me the look of 'thanks a lot'. I just smiled at him. Jennifer and I then ordered a glass of wine and next Andrew was standing beside me at the bar with his coat on. As I looked at him, the words just popped out of my mouth, "Oh my God, Andrew, you don't look very good." He then went out the side door with a friend. Jennifer and I finished our wine and we left.

I went home and I was still upset and wanting to defend myself. I thought about calling the owner of the restaurant and making a fuss but why and what good would it do.

As time has passed, we got through Christmas and New Year; the drama was still there but more tolerable. I forgave myself for being human and then I was able to use my skill of being the witness. This was the entire learnings or lesson in the situation. I was to learn to be the witness and non-reactive. The witness is when you have a situation unfolding and you pull yourself out of it and witness what is happening. This understanding of this skill helped me a lot. So as more situations unfolded around me, I was able to be non-reactive and most importantly, I was able to not take on the negative energy of the moment. I learned to walk away silently from all situations.

Love Makes You Crazy

As I reflect over the last few weeks, I wonder what happened to me as I had already done a lot of work towards a higher level of consciousness and the ability to be non-reactive. I had written books on it as well, *A Woman's Passage to Freedom,* and I was in my destiny of healing people. I was well on my way to living a conscious life but this all changed when I fell in love with Andrew and experiencing a twin flame relationship. The utopia that I experience during our times together made me forget all that I had known. I didn't care if I only had a couple hours sleep before I went to work and was driving on the highway in this condition. I didn't care if I was spending my money on someone else, I didn't care if I was only spending time with him and not being there for the people I loved. I didn't care if I was staying up to late and drinking more than I would have. I didn't care about my writing as much and I didn't care about my body either. All I wanted was to be in the feeling of love. We do know that love is the greatest feeling and it was so wonderful although balance is a key in this area as well. I just had to find love in a heart relationship that wasn't from the ego that had my thoughts in line and my emotions too. This was my final test of consciousness.

One time I was in California, over a year ago I had very bad sunburn which turned into a wonderful gift of a forced 14-hour meditation. This meditation brought me to the realisation I was not happy with the circumstances of my life. I was not happy where my love relationship had taken me. I also came to the conclusion that I was the one and only one that was responsible for exactly where I was in life. I looked in the mirror and I was not happy with my body. I looked terrible as my belly was bloated and my weight was extremely high. My bank account was low with being on holidays and my overall essence was low. I was a mess and I had put myself there. At least I had the consciousness level to recognise this and know that I was going to make a change. I knew I was out of balance and I needed to make a lot of changes to save myself once again.

It is now a year and a half later. I believe I had the answers but I was not able to apply them as application is imperative. The attachment, blind love and lack of love for me was still present in my life.

Now at this time, I started to resonate with the concept of attachment in a twin flame relationship. I knew that I had released all attachments with my other relationships; that was another reason why they were so healthy. Was I to learn non-attachment in the strongest love relationship possible?

It was a couple weeks into January that I heard Andrew wasn't doing well. He was drinking and missing shifts at work and was almost fired from his new job. Part of me thought this would be good for him, as he drank too much when he worked in places that were late night bar places. Me being me, drove up to see if he was all right. Andrew wasn't there but I talked to his roommate who told me he was okay. I informed him that I heard differently and that he was drunk all the time and not showing up for work. I then told him to tell Andrew I was here asking about him.

It was a couple weeks later that Andrew showed up on my doorstep, saying he missed me and that I was the only woman besides his first love that made him feel whole. I thought to myself, wow you have finally got it. You are finally learning to value love, value me and to pay attention to your heart and soul. He said so many wonderful things that night that I was sure he truly understood the power of love and how blessed we were to have each other. The passion we experienced that night was magnetic and magical as it always could be.

I went right back to being there for Andrew, loving him, giving to him and living a life that was not healthy for me. I just wasn't ready to get out of this lifestyle or to put my own self-love or self-worth first. Moreover, I wasn't able to be truly present in this relationship. Or maybe I hadn't healed from what Andrew was in my life to heal? Obviously I had more growth to take place. Was non-attachment to Andrew still my test?

It didn't take long for Andrew's pattern to return. Even though he had verbally said the words that he realised that our bond or relationship was one of a kind, that our bond would be there until one of us dies or that we would always be in each other lives, he still had the issues of non-commitment and loving someone.

Andrew got another job within a walking distance from where he was living in another bar situation. He seemed to be doing okay with this. I didn't go to this bar as I was spending enough time with him. This on and off relationship lasted for the next few months. I then found myself on another plane to visit my granddaughter. A strange thing happened the day I was to return home. I didn't want to get on the plane. It was extremely strange for me not wanting to go to the airport. I believe it was my subconscious wanting to get my attention. I arrived home hoping I would be strong again to break away from this relationship that had no consistency, commitment or future.

Andrew called me the moment I got off the plane and wanted to meet up with me. I had bought him a couple shirts and so I invited him over. We were home having a beer and Andrew decided he needed to get out of the environment he was living in. He then told me he wanted to live with me and be in a committed relationship with me. I was in shock and wasn't truly sure if this was a good idea but it had presented itself so I was open to it. It really was what I wanted.

We actually had the most wonderful two weeks. There was no judgment, no beliefs in the way, no roommates at this time and we were able to enjoy the love between us. We stayed in a lot and enjoyed just being together. It was the most beautiful two weeks I had ever experienced with a man.

Unfortunately, after these two weeks and a new roommate, things started to change. We were going out more and when Andrew introduced me he would say, "This is my girlfriend and she is 55 years of age." This hurt a lot because he didn't say, "This is my girlfriend; she is beautiful, smart, a writer and she loves me." I started to feel that no matter how much he loved me, he couldn't get over the age difference. His belief system was too embedded that he should be with someone is own age or the man should be older.

We went a few weeks later to the casino with another couple and the words Andrew said still haunt me. He said, "I have a 55-year-old girlfriend; how did I get stuck with her?" I knew at this time that Andrew was not able to get over the age difference. I have compassion for him as I struggled with it myself. But this was hurtful; he didn't see the beautiful woman that I was, only someone that was older than him.

He then started spending more time back with his old roommate and I started concentrating on my future as I was in financial ruins. My unemployment insurance had run out and I was borrowing money from my youngest daughter to pay my rent. I was in the midst of rewriting my script but I had to find a job. My youngest daughter suggested I go back into the restaurant business and so I put three applications out and was hired at all three places. I did attempt to work all three places at the beginning. I think Andrew was impressed with this as he was a good line cook and knew the restaurant business.

My first job was at a breakfast place and they were in such need for cooks. Knowing I was going to leave this place and that Andrew could walk to this location, I started working on a job for him. He started a few days before my last day. Life was going well at this time. We both were mirroring each other with good jobs happening and enjoying each other at the same time.

One day, we decided to go out on my sea-doo for the day and we had a fantastic time. As we were back at his place and a little drunk, Andrew decided to tell me something that would forever change our relationship. It was something he thought I should know that happened between him and his roommate's girlfriend but I didn't take it so well. We had been drinking and it was not the time to tell me something so horrible. I got upset, I slapped him across the face twice and he smashed his phone. I left knowing this was something I could never forgive him for and that it was truly over between us.

We really were two people that were from different worlds and the fact that we had survived being in each other's lives for 4.5 years was a miracle.

We continued fighting and Andrew actually blamed me and that I had done something wrong. It was his past and inability to take responsibility for his actions; this protection was in full force. Knowing he developed this as a child as his parents were very hard on him, I feel for him, as having damaging parents will affect you until you do the work to heal, understand the dysfunction and let go of it. I know that it is going to be painful without the twin flame connection and the other half of my soul, but there seems to be no other choice. Plus, if it took me hundreds of lifetimes to find my other half of my soul, then no wonder I don't want to or haven't been able to let go of Andrew.

I sit with the events that have unfolded and I know it's over. I just can't accept what Andrew did. It's time for me to move on with my life for good. I'm making money and enjoyed my job as a waitress at this new restaurant. I love the staff and the owner is wonderful.

I arrive for a Wednesday shift and I am told that the head chef that has been there for eleven years has quit. The owner then approaches me and asks me about Andrew. He asks if Andrew could come and work here with us. I listen to him as my good friend, Brenda, and her partner are friends of his and I can't believe I am hearing these words out of his mouth. I then think to myself and say to myself, "Are you kidding me?" I finally got away from him and you want me to bring him here to work? Like really universe, how could this be happening?

The owner continues throughout my shift to talk to me about Andrew coming to work here. He even says to me to take one for the team. The look on my face must have been a little shocking as there was silence for a minute and then I walk away from him. An hour later, he asks me again and I tell him I have to think about it.

The nightshift starts and due to the lack of staff in the kitchen, we are running 90-minute chit times. This means that when the food order is taken from the customer it takes 90 minutes for the food to arrive. We as a team, as a restaurant, are in very bad shape. It takes me a couple days and I say to the owner, "Okay, I will try and contact him." Over the next few days, I start talking to Andrew again. Then he is in my bed again and I have forgiven him. I never thought I would forgive but the universe was pretty right in my face that he is still to be in my life and I still love him.

At first, Andrew is not willing to come to this new restaurant because I work there and it's a 15-min drive. Although as time passes, I convince Andrew to come and help us.

Andrew does amazing on the line in the kitchen. He is an awesome line cook. The food is coming out great, the customers and the owner is very happy. Within the next few days, Andrew is offered the kitchen manager's position and he accepts. Andrew and I are now working together.

Andrew is doing well and the customers of the restaurant are recovering too. It is about a week in and all of a sudden, Andrew wants nothing to do with me. He acts as if we barely know each other and then he starts chasing one of the regular customers. I am in shock and asking God how this could be happening. Can I really go through more pain and be continually tested in such a difficult way? I then warn him about this woman as I see a lot of darkness within her. Andrew reacts to this and I get the line that I am jealous.

Andrew also, when I am working and he is off, sits with this woman for a few hours, laughing and talking to her. Every time I have to ring in an order I have to do it at the only POS that is right in front of where they are sitting. Andrew then starts to realise I am not doing well and he tries to keep this away from me. My boss and I are thankful, as it was not a nice thing to be happening to me. Andrew did tell him before he hired him that he had been intimate with me for the last three years.

I manage to survive the next few weeks and I don't know how but Andrew is still in my life. He is now staying with me, sleeping beside me but all the intimacy has left our relationship once again. He still needs me but we are not having sex anymore and I have been here before.

It's a month later and then right in front of me, he starts to date this woman. I have to work my shifts at work where I used to love my job and watch him put all his energy into another woman. I am praying for strength continually to survive this hardship.

I then end up in the bar in Midland and I met this wonderful man my age and similar to my energy. I just feel that God has sent me this wonderful man to be in my life. We continue to date and life is going great. Then everything falls apart for Andrew and this new woman. She no longer comes to the restaurant and their time together is over. Andrew starts paying attention to me again and I go right back to him. I don't know if its love, attachment, or familiarity or the fact that women want to love and we know how great the benefits are to love and I go back into a relationship with him. He is, at this time, still telling everyone we are just friends. Moreover, I push away this wonderful new man that has come into my life. I break his heart.

Next, a very sad awareness comes into my life as my sister is now on her deathbed. This becomes the hardest thing for me. I don't want her to go and I know she wants to go. Things are not good with Andrew but it's as if we put everything aside and he supports me in my time of need. We are finally enjoying some intimacy at this time as well. We are also spending a lot of time together, going to the casino, out for dinner and sleeping beside each other. That's one thing I love is Andrew sleeping beside me. It's like we have been sleeping beside each other for many years or that our souls feel content when they are close to each other. I do receive the news of my sister's passing with Andrew and my beloved cat, Ernie, beside me. Andrew says he is going to be there for me which doesn't unfold. I attend the funeral by myself.

The next week, Andrew is there for me and holding space for me once again. Then all of a sudden, he sends me these not so nice texts. He tells me we are over, that he likes some other girl and that there is no love for me and to go and see the man I had recently dated. I'm thinking to myself this is strange and maybe it could be jealousy that is the driver in this event.

A couple days pass and we on our way to the casino and Andrew is staying over again. He is back in my life as if nothing had happened. We actually spend quite a bit of time together over the next week and we get a room at the casino which I paid for and we had the most wonderful time. For being 20 years apart in age, we enjoy every minute we are together.

All of a sudden, I notice he is texting someone and I see that it is a woman. We are still at the casino and I say to myself, there is no way he could do that to me. We end up back at my place; we are sleeping and his phone goes off. He gets out of bed and I think he is in the bathroom and to my surprise, he has left. All of a sudden all the pieces fit together and I know he is going to meet with this girl the next day. I, at this time, become extremely angry. He asked me to go to the casino, asked me to get a room which I paid for, knowing he was going out on a date the next day with another woman. How much of his true colours did I need to see? How much more of this one-sided relationship did I need to encounter? How much more of the horrible treatment did I have to take before I had more self-love for myself? No matter how much I loved him, I had to be strong and I had to detach from him. So I told him I deserved more and the bond that was between Andrew and me was finally broken.

It was three days later that I had to work with Andrew and I had some not so nice words for him. I said words to him that were not good at all and I didn't care.

It has been a month now and things have remained the same with distance between Andrew and me. I got another job so I don't have to see Andrew anymore or ever again. It was an unlikely relationship in the first place as we had everything against us. Age, background, a broken soul, different beliefs and Andrew did still live his life from his ego. If he had been connected to his soul, he never would have been able to treat me so poorly or really anyone else in his life. If he was able to live from his soul, he probably would see his children. I do understand the damage and why he wasn't connected to his soul but I couldn't be involved with this anymore. I had to learn detachment from my twin flame. This was my final test of consciousness.

I am also thankful for the time, the many learnings and the experience of a twin flame but I'm very happy knowing that self-love in a relationship is key to any successful relationship. So thank you, Andrew!

Love

Now let's get back to the love part. I believe and know that love is a gift and a blessing. We are here on earth to experience love in human form but we need a lot of help in this area. Most of all, I believe in the power of love and firstly the power of love for yourself. When you have self-love, you can do anything and nothing will stand in your way. Your relationships are all strong as you have no negative limitations within them.

Now I have only felt love for a man four times in my life and I am grateful for all of them. I believe when you are in balance and in a loving relationship with a partner, you both will be unstoppable.

I believed unconditional love would solve everything and I was wrong. I was losing myself and my life by giving total unconditional love without self-love. I still believe in love and I know the power of it and it must come with boundaries and self-love. When this is all in place, it is when the miracles start to happen. I see this right now with my daughters. The love the three of us have right now is very special and it's creating such wonderful miracles in all our lives.

This love is unconditional, as we have no demands or judgment on each other. This love is from the heart and soul so the ego is not existent. Moreover, we all exercise self-love in this relationship. I support as a mother should, without judgment or criticism, as it's their journeys; it's magical within our relationships. We all have boundaries, we listen to each other, we support each other, there is no ego in our relationships and this is the true power of love.

I do believe I had a lot of fear in my relationship with Andrew and this was the ego at work. I had fear of losing him or losing the feeling that was so amazing which caused attachment and the Runner/Chaser scenario. I brought myself down to his level and lost my life because of it. I lost my balance also because of it. There was love and there still is and if another chance comes along, our relationship will be much different. I will understand the love and remove the fear and attachment to any other man that I love. I am trying to release the attachment to Andrew with now sending him love and wishing him greatness in his life. I have compassion for him as well. I am maintaining my boundaries and what is important to me. If this happens, I will be more of a true mirror for each other as we are really one big mirror reflecting everything back and forth. I have remembered that self-love is so much a part of everything, as you cannot have love until you have self-love. These are the lessons and the learning for the growth I needed to learn in this twin flame relationship.

Just Stay in Alignment

This beautiful message I would like to say that I give credit to Abraham, or Ester, and Jerry Hicks as this is what I am hearing from them and it is working for me. The first time I heard this message from them, it was in concern with Jesus and how He was able to master this skill and stay in the alignment of the vortex. That He was no different than you and me, as I believe this He just was able to master being in the vibration of love at all times. He was able to master living life from his soul. He was able to eliminate his ego. Therefore I take this message and guidance to stay in alignment of the vortex and the love of God.

Attachment

I am struggling once again with the bond I have for Andrew. It's very painful and I don't feel whole without him but I am not seeing him, although I am still texting him on occasion. I don't know for sure if he has blocked me but I am still attached to him. Therefore, I return to YouTube for more knowledge and assistance.

First I find information on attachment that we are to learn non-attachment in the most powerful love relationships. This means to be happy if your twin flame is in your life or not and to wish him or her love and peace on their journeys. This was difficult and something I had to learn and master. I had to release the attachment to Andrew. I prayed to be able to release him and then I deleted his contact information out of my phone so I couldn't contact him. Next I meditated on the release of Andrew with the love remaining. I knew there was no way the love was going to leave and I was accepting this. This worked for me. It was a change in my essence and it felt good and powerful.

Next I find this beautiful video on the purpose of a twin flame and this is what I learned. God has created us as a twin flame for us to learn, grow and evolve to our point of origin as perfected beings. We are to create truer love in the world, as this love is very powerful. This love is an awaking of the soul and our purpose is to awaken other souls. To reunite with your twin flame, you must reach a state of unconditional love for yourself and your twin flame. This is to love without condition, to talk without intention, to give without reason and to care without expectation; this being the spirit of true love. This love is also accepting the dark and the light and to balance it within to become one. You are to create divine oneness with God, to restore the unity within mankind and to find your soul.

This is to eliminate the ego in a true love union and to find 'Self-Love'. Yay, this is what I learned! I had to find self-love! To really love myself from the inside out! I still believe you can have a relationship with unconditional love, no judgement a love without conditions but it must go hand and hand with self-love!

Twin flames are to raise the consciousness of mankind. This has already been my purpose in this lifetime. Twins are to be in spiritual service to God, mankind and to cause awakenings in others from their egos to their souls. To dissolve the ego by letting go of the need to control, old belief systems and programming of society and the low vibrations and negativity! Are you prepared to serve?

OMG, this is truly and OMG moment. I have experienced and written all of this. I know all of this as truth. This is one of the reasons I became the chaser.

I have been serving for many years and many lifetimes but I have no idea if Andrew is ready to serve mankind or the divine. A twin flame relationship is androgynous relationship. You adapt to be one. You are to help with the ascension of the planet.

Conclusion

With all I know from my learnings and my teachings about relationships, this is my conclusion. I have also asked for help from my guides, God and the inner knowledge that I have from my past lives to this very moment to write this final chapter. So here we go!

Firstly, what if everything we know about relationships is not true. We seem to hear this daily with this being the year 2019, the year of truth, that everything we know about the world is a lie. We are told these lies are being told to us to keep us small and in slave mentality, so why would this not pertain to our thoughts and beliefs on how and what our relationships should took like or be. What if we completely changed our perspective on our relationships? One thing we know for sure is that our relationships haven't been working. We are experiencing much more dysfunction in our relationships then we ever have had. It magnifies this beliefs a hundred times more. We do need to remember the guidelines from the 10 commandments though. Treat each other as we would like to be treated, respect each other, no adultery and no stealing. Those are our ground rules in all areas of life.

Let's review the learning from the beginning of the book with all relationships. We have our parents that we pick to learn from. They are our teachers and we are to see this perspective and know to let go of some and keep others close. Our children are here for us to teach and protect but they are always on their own journeys. We are to be their friends but first and foremost, we are to be their parents. Being a parent means to teach what is right from wrong, to teach spirituality, to live from example, to respect them as we wish to be respected and to love them. We are to give our children our time and be present for them.

Now let's start on the love relationships. Firstly, we are not to expect anyone else to make us happy or even try to place that burden or job on someone else. I have heard the saying, "I want to make her happy." Well, forget that right now as you can't. Happiness lies within and can only individually be found by you and only you. If you think a relationship is going to complete you, then think again. A relationship is to enhance the person that you are. For you women out there, no man is to make you happy; you have to do this all by yourself. Plus, if you are in a relationship trying to make someone else happy, stop right now because you will lose your individuality and your authentic self. I know from my personal experiences this will not work at all.

Love belief systems. I know for sure that none of these belief systems that I have held within over the last 40 years has worked for me. Therefore, I am going to change my perspective on relationships. Everything is all about perspective anyways and when you change your perspective, everything around you changes and let me tell you it can be extremely powerful.

Now from what I have learned and experienced and from my insight, the most important relationship you have is with yourself and with God. It's your spirituality that you have within that makes all your relationships healthy. This is really the key. Once I worked on my spirituality and myself, all my relationships became healthy. This also had a lot to do with me not self-betraying myself, or self-sabotaging myself, letting go of the unhealthy belief systems and getting out of the pattern of the ego. Perfect example is with my sister, Anne. The unhealthy belief system was that we were to be close and as soon as I let that go, in time, we actually became close. I just accepted what it was and continued on with my journey. I'm actually going to try this right now with Andrew. He's young and has a lot of life lessons to learn. Me, wanting more from him or wanting him to be a certain way or expecting him to be in a committed relationship is wrong. He has his own life; therefore, this being another belief system that didn't serve me well at all in the love relationship.

All relationships are not perfect because there is no such thing as a perfect anything and as long as there in no abuse or anyone being hurt, then they all have different forms, especially love relationships. We are just experiencing too much programming by the media, TV and movies. Just follow your heart and listen. Do not let you head control your heart. I see it all the times with our youth. "You have to be with me all the time." How did we get to that point?

I also thank Andrew for being this awareness to me at this time in my life. Maybe the sword that came down was the sword of stop trying to hard or wanting something that is just not possible at this time. Maybe it will be in another year, who knows. The basics of living in the now also retains to love or romantic relationships. So just take it day at a time and let it unfold. Plus, I don't really want to lose myself in a love relationship at all in any way. I just spent years finding myself. Most of all, the power I was giving over to Andrew was crazy and I was giving it freely. He did take some of my power but I gave it mostly over to him all by myself. I was a little excited though because my soul was alive and it had been a long time since I felt that way.

So now I have the answer of why God sent me Andrew. Andrew has brought so much growth to me in my love relationship area and I am so very thankful for our time together.

If we only thanked all the lovers we have had over the course of our lifetimes. To just sit in the love we had because there is always some love and see the growth we experienced. I am letting go of all the not-so-good belief systems that were in place in my head or as we truly know it to be, our ego. I truly believe that my next encounter with love, with it being with Andrew or another man, will be one that will not be led by the ego. The ego also creates attachment which is a not good thing in any relationship. My next relationship will be a relationship from the soul.

Now a message to the men, embrace love as it doesn't come along to often in a lifetime. Open your hearts and your emotions to love. Love is the most powerful essence on earth and we need to know it, understand it and value it.

Now for all of us, communication is also extremely important. We need remember to say how you feel and to be open to how the other person feels. They and we are allowed to feel this way. Mankind has swallowed their emotions for so many years then to have it became a slap in the face. Let it out before it becomes a volcano that spills everywhere and lastly, remember life is a highway and prepare for the low times, the disagreements and the flat tires. They are, for sure, going to take place. That's why we are here, to learn from our journey and our ups and downs. I, too, am human and I must always be aware of my thoughts and emotions with evaluation if are they from the ego or the soul. I also have let go of a lot of un-serving patterns..

What I have learned and what has worked for me and what I now go by and live by, I call it the JC Code of living, JC meaning Jesus Christ. I discovered through my experiences the more I personal adapted the teachings, and the way of being of Jesus the healthier my relationships became. His teachings being, non-judgemental, no blame, controlling my negative emotions and thoughts, no control over others, being kind to others ,being in service, treating others the way I wanted to be treated, accepting what is, being non-reactive, no attachment and most of all self-love. Being just like JC made all my relationships healthy. I now also understand why it says in the bible the only way to God is through Jesus Christ. This is because you find the love of God and are the love of God when you are like Jesus.

Relationships are everywhere and constant, from the neighbours you wave to, to the clerk at the grocery store, to the people you work with, to your friends, to your family, to yourself, to your lover and to God. Life is really just a whole lot of RELATIONSHIPS!

ormation can be obtained
testing.com
USA
20321
2B/288